T0287743

Let It Settle

Let It Settle

DAILY HABITS *to* MOVE YOU
from CHAOS *to* CALM

MICHAEL GALYON

WILEY

Published by John Wiley & Sons, Inc., Hoboken, New Jersey.
Published simultaneously in Canada.

For general information on our other products and services or for technical support, please contact our Customer Care Department within the United States at (800) 762-2974, outside the United States at (317) 572-3993 or fax (317) 572-4002.

Wiley also publishes its books in a variety of electronic formats. Some content that appears in print may not be available in electronic formats. For more information about Wiley products, visit our web site at www.wiley.com.

Library of Congress Cataloging-in-Publication Data

Names: Galyon, Michael, author.
Title: Let it settle : daily habits to move you from chaos to calm /
  Michael Galyon.
Description: Hoboken, New Jersey : Wiley, [2024] | Includes index.
Identifiers: LCCN 2024025043 (print) | LCCN 2024025044 (ebook) | ISBN
  9781394196142 (hardback) | ISBN 9781394196166 (adobe pdf) | ISBN
  9781394196173 (epub)
Subjects: LCSH: Calmness. | Mindfulness (Psychology) | Meditation.
Classification: LCC BF575.C35 G36 2024 (print) | LCC BF575.C35 (ebook) |
  DDC 158.1/3—dc23/eng/20240705
LC record available at https://lccn.loc.gov/2024025043
LC ebook record available at https://lccn.loc.gov/2024025044

Cover Design: Wiley
Cover Image: © nadtytok/iStock/Getty Images

SKY10082530_082624

For you

Contents

Calm Kit Tools

Tool	Chapter
#1: 5-4-3-2-1 Calming Technique for Anxiety	1
#2: Body Scan	2
#3: Butterfly Hug	3
#4: Gremlin Discovery Technique	5
#5: Self-Love Guided Visualization	6
#6: Calm Space Visualization	7
#7: Self-Compassion Journal	8
#8: Nonjudgment Practice	10
#9: Anger RAID Meditation	11
#10: Loving-Kindness (Metta) Meditation	12
#11: Forgiveness Meditation	13

Meditations

Meditation	Chapter
Body Scan Meditation	4
Four-Point Breathing Meditation	4
Safe Space Meditation	4
Mindful Awareness of Thought Meditation	9
Self-Love Meditation	9
Heart-Centered Meditation	9
Anger RAID Meditation	14
Loving-Kindness (Metta) Meditation	14
Forgiveness Meditation	14

Daily Habits

Habit	Chapter
Daily Practice of Mindful Awareness	4
Daily Mindfulness Breaks	4
Daily Stress Reduction Techniques	4
Daily Self-Reflection Practice	9
Daily Intention-Setting Practice	9
Daily Acts of Self-Care	9
Daily Exploration of Empathy	14
Daily Practice of Loving-Kindness	14
Daily Practice of Letting Go	14

Preface: Unsettled

I remember the love I felt from holding my grandmother's hand and knowing how much I was cared for, the excitement of that first glimpse of the mountains from the backseat of our van on family road trips to Colorado, the anger that filled my body when my older brother teased me, the loneliness that came from being a shy kid without many friends, and the heartbreak that came from watching my mom walk out the door to start a new life away from us when I was nine. I felt everything so deeply, sometimes I didn't know how to keep it inside my body. While it may not have been what little boys were supposed to do in those days, I was never too shy to feel everything and express it fully.

But on the day my mom left, something shifted. I had spent the morning listening to her preparations, packing up items that had been in our home my entire life and leaving empty spaces outlined in dust. I wasn't entirely aware of what was going on, but I knew that this was different from other times she had left. There were many moments leading up to this day when I sat behind my closed bedroom door listening to raised voices and trying to figure out what was being said, praying that it would end so I could stop feeling so scared and everything would be OK. When my parents finally sat us down to let us know that she was leaving, I didn't quite understand what it meant. It wasn't until that day, watching her things leave with her, that I started to grasp what was happening.

When the last items were packed and she was ready to leave, my siblings and I lined up, and she hugged each of us good-bye. I was the last one to hug her, and by that time, the tears had started to fall. The weight of what was happening settled in, and being the sensitive boy that I was, I let myself feel everything. When she looked and saw the tears rolling down my face, she turned to me, holding back her own tears, and softly said, "No more tears. I need you to be my brave little soldier." Then she walked out the door, and my tears stopped for many years.

After decades of work on both of our parts and a beautiful reconciliation, I can see now that her words were more for her than for me. The intense pain of a choice that she knew was necessary but impacted so many was too much, and she just wanted her little boy to be OK without her. But at that moment, the message I took away was that feelings I once felt so freely were no longer safe. For years I held on to those words and did everything I could to distance myself from the intense emotions I felt and be the "brave little soldier" I thought I needed to be. That abandonment of my emotions left everything in my life seeming unsettled. No matter what I was experiencing, there was a deep longing to escape it. I yearned to escape the pain and discomfort of difficult moments as well as the moments of joy and happiness for fear that the fall from those emotional heights would hurt too badly. I constantly tried to control situations to find a place of neutrality—a space where I could exist devoid of emotion. That sensitive boy who felt everything suddenly became a man who sought to feel nothing.

There were many ways to achieve this state of nothing-ness, and behind closed doors and away from the image of the brave little soldier I was sharing with the world, I experi-enced almost all of them to excess. Through a cycle of restric-tion and abuse of food, hiding behind career success, alcohol, and countless other addictions, distractions, and obsessions, I tried to distance myself from the emotions that raged in me. I was constantly searching for the next thing to take away this unsettled feeling, but it always came up short. Even after sobriety, I leaned into more socially acceptable obsessions like fitness, yoga, and meditation. I wish that I could say my pursuit of mindfulness and meditation was an attempt to deepen my experience of life and begin to feel into it all, but initially it was another form of escape. It was almost as if the stillness and silence of a meditation replaced the dissociative quality of the coping mechanisms I had relied on earlier to escape those feelings. As embarrassing as it is to admit, for many years my practice existed solely to avoid feeling.

But eventually the stillness and silence of meditation and the conscious awareness provided by mindfulness allowed for the walls surrounding these emotions to begin to come down. Over time I was able to settle into a space where I could let them be present, feel them, and finally begin to process what I had been avoiding for so long. To let every-thing settle, I had to first unlearn what had been taught to me and find my way back to that sensitive little boy. As with most things that enact change, it didn't happen overnight. It was a process of deconstructing old beliefs, building new habits, and allowing myself to find calm amid the chaos.

The first belief that I had to deconstruct was that stoicism was a way to earn love. Throughout my life adults praised me for being that brave little soldier and for my ability to remain neutral in the face of any and all situations. I misconstrued this praise as love, and therefore created a firm belief that the more stoic I was, the more love I would receive. It made perfect sense and often provided me with the feeling I was seeking, but the cost of burying my emotions became apparent as time went by. For years I would people-please, ignore my own feelings and needs, and become what others wanted me to be in fear that if my emotions slipped out, the love and attention I had received would be taken away. Stepping away from that pattern of behavior was terrifying and seemed impossible most days. When the conscious awareness of how I was showing up and the impact it was having on my life finally became clear to me, I knew that, to move forward, I needed to start connecting with my emotions and return home to myself.

On this journey home to myself, I tried countless forms of therapy, self-help seminars, books, religious teachings, and anything I could think of. Although many of them made an impact, the simplicity of awareness through mindfulness-based meditation and practices gave me the ability to start understanding myself on a deeper level and create choice for how I wanted to show up for myself in the world. Starting and ending each day in reflection and tuning in to my body, my breath, my thoughts, and my emotions allowed me to see who I was separate from the image I portrayed for others. It allowed me the opportunity to sit with feelings of discomfort, fear, and loneliness, and let them be present without judgment. It allowed me to recognize that it was safe to feel and that expressing those feelings would not keep others from loving me.

Over time, a deep sense of calm replaced the stoicism I had felt. I learned to remain calm in the face of fear, not in avoidance of it. As I started showing up for myself and connecting more deeply with the people in my life, I started to become aware of small reference points to confirm that there was safety in expression and that love didn't disappear in the face of feelings. Once I was able to recognize that, I was able to begin to let it all settle and find my way forward.

Next I had to break down the belief that safety was possible only when hiding behind a mask of perceived perfection and when giving people only what they wanted from me. I thought I had to be the perfect doll for them to play with, to meet their needs, to understand them, and to create a space where conflict could not exist. The more I began to connect with myself and my emotions, I recognized that the connections in my life were dependent on a falsified version of peace. With that came resentment, unvoiced pain, and an inability to truly connect with people in my life. The process of deconstructing this belief took time and energy and required me to look at my own way of relating to the people in my life. It forced me to learn how to empathize on a deep level, to learn how to forgive, to learn how to be in conflict, and to learn how to love. It wasn't one specific moment that taught me the lessons I needed to learn, but a collection of teachings spread over years that all culminated in my ability to take off the mask and enter into healthy relationships.

Finally, I needed to learn how to be connected with the world around me. I need to step away from the comfort of self-focus and let myself find a vision that served the world around me by simply showing up authentically and with purpose. Throughout my life I always tended to play small and place myself in a box. I was too scared to make noise or be seen, and I continually scanned the world to see how I could fit in but not stand out. I strove to learn the rules and carefully studied the actions of others to know what was expected of me. In doing so, I was denying a part of myself. Learning to come home to myself and connect to those closest to me allowed me finally to begin to let things flow through me, not from me. In that openness, I found a desire to create a kinder, calmer, and more connected world. When I shifted the focus from how I wanted to be perceived by others to how I wanted to show up for others, I was able to create that vision for my life and find ways to have that lead me forward with purpose and drive.

In service of that vision, I've devoted the last decade to helping others find their calm. My hope is that this book can be a source of inspiration and knowledge that will help guide you home to yourself and finally begin to let it all settle.

Michael Galyon
March 2024

Introduction

I wish that I could say that with a few simple breaths and a focus on the present moment, you can solve all of life's problems. In reality, finding calm amid the chaos is an ongoing process, and at times fear and anxiety will win the day. The intention of this book is not to simply gather the tools of mindfulness, find the right meditative practices, and create the perfect daily habits to reach a permanent place of peace. That place does not exist, and chaos will continue to creep into your life from time to time, regardless of the tools you discover within these pages.

My hope is that the tools, tips, and practices we'll uncover together will give you the strength to keep moving through life no matter how many storms come your way. The information in this book is there to help you through whatever storm you're facing right now. That storm may be a lack of calm within your life, a feeling of disconnection from yourself, or the difficulties that come from being in conflict with those you hold dearest. Whatever you are facing right now is a unique and personal journey, but I hope you can see yourself in some of the stories presented here and find some solace knowing you are not alone. There are things you can do to help you let it all settle and, for a moment, find some calm in the chaos.

How This Book Is Organized

I've broken the following pages into the three areas that led me on my path. They will help as you begin your journey of moving from chaos to calm.

> **Part 1: Finding Calm** is about finding calm within your life and facing the inner blocks that are holding you back and keeping you stuck in unhealthy patterns.
>
> **Part 2: Coming Home to Yourself** is about recognizing your unique and inherent goodness and connecting back with an authentic version of yourself.
>
> **Part 3: Honoring Connection** is about creating deep and meaningful relationships with the people in your life and breaking through the blocks that may be standing in your way.

Chapters in each part of this book highlight some of life's bigger challenges. The goal of these chapters is to provide you with specific tools, practices, or methods you can utilize as you move through the challenges outlined in the chapter. Using storytelling, I take you through my own personal experiences and through my work with clients to showcase these tools in action and show movement from one side of the challenge to the other.

> All names, experiences, and events have been changed and do not represent any one person.

How to Use This Book's Tools

Each chapter ends with a step-by-step guide on how to utilize the process outlined in the chapter in your own life. It also provides a specific tool that you can add to what I affectionately call your Calm Kit, an ever-growing collection of calming tools that you can pull from to help ground you back into the present moment and begin to find calm amid the chaos.

The chapters at the end of each of the three parts—Chapters 4, 9, and 14—contain written meditations to help you move through the challenges presented in each chapter in that part. Reach for these meditations in times of need or incorporate them into your daily practice.

Additionally, Chapters 4, 9, and 14 provide you with a set of daily habits to help keep you grounded and prevent you from straying too far from a centered space of calm and stillness. These daily habits, along with the exercises found at the end of each chapter that create your Calm Kit, serve as inspiration to turn to when you begin to lose your way.

Preparing for Meditation

Meditation offers a variety of benefits for both mental and physical well-being. Regular practice can significantly reduce stress by lowering cortisol levels and promoting relaxation. It enhances focus and concentration, leading to improved productivity and cognitive function. Emotionally, meditation fosters stability, resilience, and inner peace, alleviating symptoms of anxiety and depression. It has also been shown to deepen self-awareness, helping practitioners better understand thoughts, emotions, and behaviors.

The practice of meditation also aids in achieving better sleep quality by calming the mind and reducing racing thoughts. By strengthening the mind–body connection, meditation promotes holistic health and harmony between physical and mental states. Ultimately, meditation contributes to an overall improved quality of life by fostering mental clarity, emotional balance, and physical health.

A Note About Mindfulness-Based Practices

The mindfulness practices that I teach, including those rooted in Buddhist traditions, are adapted and practiced in a secular context. In secular mindfulness, the emphasis is on the practical application of mindfulness techniques for enhancing well-being, managing stress, and promoting emotional regulation; the aim is not to explore metaphysical realms or experiences, or religious or spiritual beliefs.

Although mindfulness-based practices originated in ancient traditions, secular mindfulness removes any religious or cultural context and focuses solely on the techniques themselves and their benefits. This approach allows individuals from diverse backgrounds to access and benefit from mindfulness without feeling the need to adhere to specific religious teachings or beliefs. By honoring and acknowledging the traditions from which these practices derive, while also offering them in a secular and accessible manner, I can ensure that mindfulness remains inclusive and applicable to all, regardless of their religious or cultural affiliations.

For beginners, sometimes the idea of meditation feels intimidating. The prospect of sitting in silence with one's thoughts may evoke feelings of discomfort or uncertainty. However, it's important to recognize that meditation doesn't have to be complex or overwhelming. In fact, the simplicity of the practice is one of its greatest strengths.

At its core, meditation is about cultivating presence and awareness in the present moment. It's not about emptying the mind or achieving a state of perfect calm; rather, it's about observing the thoughts, sensations, and emotions that arise without judgment or attachment. Understanding this fundamental principle can help alleviate some of the anxiety beginners may feel about meditation.

To set yourself up for success with meditation, establish a consistent habit that fits into your daily routine. Start small, perhaps with just a few minutes of meditation each day, and gradually increase the duration as you become more comfortable with the practice. Choose a time and place where you can meditate without distractions, and experiment with different techniques to find what works best for you.

Consistency is key when it comes to meditation. Just like any other skill, meditation requires practice and patience to develop. By committing to regular meditation practice, you can gradually build your mindfulness muscle and begin to experience the benefits of meditation in your daily life.

It's also important to approach meditation with an open mind and a sense of curiosity. Don't be discouraged by the inevitable distractions or challenges that may arise during meditation. Instead, view them as opportunities for growth and learning. Remember that meditation is a journey, and each moment of practice brings you closer to greater clarity, peace, and self-awareness.

Consider these six steps to help you create a consistent practice of meditation:

1. **Find your space.** Choose a quiet and comfortable space where you can practice meditation without distractions. This doesn't need to be a dedicated meditation room, and you don't need to purchase expensive meditation cushions. To this day I still sit on the edge of my couch

for my meditation sessions. The important thing is to make sure that it's somewhere where you feel relaxed and at ease.

2. **Settle into a comfortable position.** Find a comfortable seated position on a cushion, chair, couch, or bench. Keep your back straight—place a cushion behind you if you need the support—and rest your hands gently in your lap. You can also lie down if that feels more comfortable, although be mindful not to fall asleep.

3. **Close your eyes or soften your gaze.** During meditation, you can choose to either close your eyes or maintain a soft gaze looking downward without focusing specifically on anything, whichever feels most natural and safe for you. When I guide meditations, I tell people that it's OK to meditate with open eyes, if closing their eyes does not feel safe or comfortable. If you choose to keep your eyes open, focus on a spot on the floor a few feet in front of you and allow your gaze to soften.

4. **Take a few deep breaths.** Take a few deep breaths to center yourself and bring your awareness into the present moment. Inhale deeply through your nose, feeling your abdomen expand, and exhale fully through your mouth, releasing any tension or stress you may be holding onto. If you need more focus, you can simply track each breath by silently saying "I am aware of my inhale, I am aware of my exhale."

5. **Let go of expectations.** Release any expectations or judgments you may have about your meditation practice. Remember that there is no right or wrong way to meditate, and each session is going to be a completely unique experience. Simply allow yourself to be present with whatever arises, without trying to force or control

your experience. And always remember that you are not a "bad meditator" if/when your mind begins to wander. Don't think of meditation as requiring a blank mind but as a practice of awareness where you note the thoughts that arise and make the conscious choice to redirect your attention to the present moment (breath, body, senses, etc.).

6. **Be patient and gentle with yourself.** Be patient and gentle with yourself as you navigate your meditation practice. Understand that meditation is a skill that takes time and practice to develop, and that progress may not always be linear. Treat yourself with kindness and compassion, and celebrate the fact that you are taking the time to invest in yourself during this time.

Cultivating Daily Habits

As you work toward finding a space of calm to return to, many practices, meditations, and techniques will prove beneficial on your journey, but don't overwhelm yourself by trying to add too much too soon. A manageable daily practice with simple habits and tools will serve you well in the long run. The daily habits that you'll find within this book are suggestions to help you move through specific challenges and can be added into your daily practice as needed. Remember that consistency is key; even just a few minutes of meditation or mindfulness each day can make a significant difference over time. Be patient with yourself and allow your practice to evolve naturally, adjusting as needed to suit your needs and preferences. With dedication and perseverance, you'll gradually cultivate a greater sense of calm, clarity, and well-being in your life.

I want to give you a gentle reminder as you work your way through the book: None of this is easy, but experiencing life instead of trying to control it is a beautiful thing, and living fully aware and present for every moment in your life is a gift worth giving to yourself. Let's get you there.

PART 1

Finding Calm

1 Letting It Settle

A Gentle Reminder

There's a lot going on in the world today, and if you've been feeling a heightened sense of emotion lately, I want you to know that you're not alone. The demands on adults today personally and professionally can be overwhelming, because we exist in a time when a constant stream of information tells us what is wrong, warns of dangers and threats, and puts us all in a state of confusion and worry. You're expected to be so much for so many, and often it can feel like no matter how hard you try, it's never enough. All of this contributes to a feeling of unease, and the level of anxiety that exists daily can be overwhelming. Given everything going on around you, you may have no concept of calm. The thought of stillness may seem foreign, and while you know that something needs to shift, you don't know how to move yourself toward a life of ease.

Most of us share a feeling of unrest, unease, and uncertainty about how to handle our emotions. It's a feeling that we're too much, too little, too angry, or too scared; that we're living in the extremes and never knowing who we are supposed to be. Beneath that unsettled feeling is a desire for peace, for stillness, for calm.

Finding a space of calm is more necessary than ever. Between information overload brought on by social media and 24-hour news sources, increased demands for productivity, a breakdown of the boundaries between personal and professional life, and rising levels of stress and anxiety, it's essential to carve out moments of calm to preserve our mental and emotional health. I know it may not seem possible right now, but my hope is that by exploring the tools and techniques presented in this book, you can begin to find a way to connect back to yourself, become aware of what's going on internally, and gain the strength to be gentle with yourself through it all. None of this is easy, and some of the tools and techniques I share may not work for you. Finding calm is a process of trial and error and requires a great deal of patience. You're asking yourself to rewrite decades of learned behavior and beliefs, so if you find yourself frustrated, that's OK. But your peace is worth fighting for, and my hope is that together we can get you one step closer toward the peaceful existence you deserve.

Understanding the Power of Letting It Settle

A signature phrase that I often use while guiding meditations and in my coaching sessions is "let it settle." I'm often asked to explain the exact meaning of the phrase. It's an invitation for you to allow your mind to find a place of rest, your body to relax, and your emotions to become less charged. The meaning of "let it settle" is quite simple, but where the phrase comes from is a much more interesting story. It doesn't come from any tenets of mindfulness or training that I received; rather, it comes from my time spent in a preschool classroom.

Before gaining my certifications as a professional coach and a mindfulness instructor, I spent more than a decade working with children. I often tell clients that the majority of what I know and what I pass on to them comes from my time in a preschool classroom. The work that we do as adults to find emotional regulation is similar to working with children, who are bundles of emotion trying to navigate through life.

It was in a preschool classroom where I learned the power of letting it settle from a three-year-old named Jack. I met Jack and his family on the first day of his new preschool separation program. This was the first time that Jack was going to be away from his family for an extended period of time, so it was a big deal for him. He walked in holding his mom's hand, and his big blue eyes lit up as he saw the room filled with color and toys and kids. I greeted them and introduced myself, pointing out all the areas Jack could explore. While still holding on to his mom's hand, he went over to the brightly colored alphabet rug and began to play. He reached for a car and started to zoom it along the rug, making sure to yell "beep beep" when he passed anyone and to make crashing noises as he bumped his toy into the car of another child. The two boys laughed as they began to play together, slowly venturing away from the adults but glancing back every few moments to make sure that the mothers were still there. After a few minutes, when Jack seemed fully engaged and comfortable, his mom decided to say good-bye and leave the room. If you're a parent who has gone through the initial separation process, you know that it's not always easy. With a swift kiss and promise that she'd be right outside, Jack's mom made her way to the door.

I could see a rush of emotions come over Jack as he watched his mom walk toward the door. I watched as the toy car dropped from his hands and the physical manifestation of fear became apparent as his body became tense, his face started to flush, and a flood of tears came. For Jack, his whole world had just changed. In the absence of his mother's comforting and safe presence, no toy in the world could distract him from his fear. In this unfamiliar place of fear, the only thing he could do was let the tears fall and rush toward the door to return to his place of safety.

Often in those moments an adult's instinct is to distract a child, to create a spectacle that would be so enticing that they would forget about their fear and join in on the fun. Occasionally that works, but it's not what Jack needed that day. In fact, the sensory overload of our attempted distraction was causing more stress for him and leading him further into panic. With each attempt we made to distract him, Jack grew more focused on his fear, and his sole intention was to return to that space of safety in his mother's arms.

I sat with Jack for several minutes trying to be as present as possible and to calm and soothe him. I hoped that he would begin to find a way to settle down, but it was clear that he just wasn't ready that day and was going to need a more gradual separation process. I went into the hallway and discussed the situation with his mom and had her come back into the classroom. The moment she walked through the door, Jack rushed to her side and clung on even tighter than before. He sank into her, and in his return to safety his temperature dropped, his breath became less shallow, the tears stopped, and eventually he was able to find his way back to the rug, grabbing the race car and zooming along.

After class Jack's mom and I discussed how to best move forward. Together we came up with a plan for me to work with both of them and discover ways to help Jack find safety and security in the space. Our goal was to eventually, when the time was right, work toward a full separation during the class.

Over the next few weeks, we tried a lot of different strategies with varying degrees of success. What finally helped Jack find comfort and safety in the classroom was a process that involved some of the mindfulness techniques I had practiced on my own in times of stress.

Learning to Settle

Teaching preschool wasn't what I had planned to do when I moved to New York. I graduated from college with a degree in music and relocated to the city to pursue a career on Broadway. Shortly after arriving there, I was fortunate enough to be cast in several musical productions around the world; one included singing with an orchestra touring China. It was an amazing opportunity to explore a foreign country and perform each night in front of large crowds with a full orchestra behind me. In fact, it had been what I had dreamed of since I performed in my first musical in sixth grade. But while it was the realization of a dream, it was also the start of a series of severe anxiety attacks.

Many nights on that tour I sat in my dressing room unable to breathe and on the verge of tears. I forced myself to go on stage to perform, then I went back to my hotel and experienced the anxiety all through the night. I kept this anxiety inside and didn't tell anyone, but fear of it happening again finally forced me to decide to step away from performing and give up that part of my life. By doing so, I lost something I cared deeply about. I recognized that I had to find ways to deal with my anxiety.

Eventually I found a meditation class, where I learned the power of presence and grounding in times of stress and anxiety. While sitting in a yoga studio in Queens, New York, I found the technique that allowed me to calm myself during anxious moments. On one particularly anxious evening, Yuval, my meditation teacher, guided us through an open-eyed meditation that brought attention to our senses and began to teach a grounding technique called the 5-4-3-2-1 Calming Technique for Anxiety. We began by bringing our attention first to five things that we could see in that moment and then shifting our awareness to four things that we could touch. Next we explored three things that we could hear and then two things we could smell. Finally, Yuval invited us to find one thing that we could taste. This exploration of the senses brought me back into the present. For the first time in months, my breath no longer felt labored, and a sense of calm washed over me. I could let my mind stop running and settle into that moment, feeling a safety I hadn't felt in a long time.

That simple exercise became a consistent practice of mine in times of stress and was the first tool in my "Calm Kit." It also happened to be the exact tool that Jack needed to begin to conquer his fears and gain independence in the classroom.

Grounding in the Present Moment

At work, I'd start each day by sitting with Jack as he said good-bye to his mom. Although over time he had gained a lot of trust and felt comfortable in the classroom, the initial shock of watching her leave always caused Jack stress. I'd give him the space to feel into those big emotions without trying to make them go away, distract him from them, or imply they were wrong in any way. I was simply there to be with him. Then I would begin to acknowledge what he was going through. I would give his emotions a name and let him know that it was OK to feel them. I'd tell him that it's OK to feel scared, it's OK to feel sad, and it makes sense that those feelings are there. When I noticed his emotions starting to settle, we would begin to find ways to return the present moment and explore all of his senses.

Using the 5-4-3-2-1 Calming Technique for Anxiety, I'd have him begin to look around the room and find five things of interest that he could see—a blue rug, 1; a red firetruck outside the window, 2; the white clock on the wall, 3; Mr. Michael's brown hair, 4; and Jack's red race car shirt, 5. Next, we'd explore four things that he could touch, noting how each one felt: the soft feeling of shaggy purple carpet, 1; the smooth feeling of the art table, 2; the bumpy feeling of the race car wheels, 3; and the slimy feeling of the Play-Doh in his hands, 4. Searching for three sounds Jack could hear in the room, we would listen carefully and hear the clock ticking on the wall, 1; the garbage truck picking up the trash outside on the street, 2; and the Baby Shark song playing on repeat from the stereo, 3. With a big breath in through his nose, we'd search for two things that Jack could smell: the yummy smell of cupcakes on the counter, 1; and yes, most days if he was feeling silly, Mr. Michael's stinky feet, 2. Finally we'd get to walk over to the table and pick between two different snacks he had brought that day and decide which one thing he wanted to taste. On most days it was his favorite, Goldfish, 1.

With that final connection to his senses, Jack would start to step away from the fear and come back to the present. In that moment of present awareness, he was able to recognize the safety and comfort of the space he was in, and everything would start to relax. His body would soften, the tears would stop, his mind would stop racing, and he'd simply let it all settle. From there he would be able to experience everything that was around him and find the excitement of what was right there the whole time.

Moving Beyond Preschool

I always held on to the image of watching Jack settle into the moment and seeing that fear melt away. Years later when I started coaching, a corporate coaching client came into her first session and broke down. She had been holding on so tightly, pushing through the fear and anxiety to succeed, and although her life appeared perfect from the outside, internally she was struggling with something she couldn't understand. When given the opportunity to put words to what she was feeling, the floodgates opened, and she started to cry. In that moment, I saw her entering a state of fear and watched as her body and breath reacted to that fear. It was so similar to Jack watching his mother leave the room that first day, but this time the client was an adult who seemed to have it all. I sat with her and let her feel into her emotions for a moment, not trying to distract her or put any pressure on her to move away from her pain. I acknowledged her feelings, giving her permission to simply let herself be with them, and validated what she was going through. The pressure of the responsibilities placed on her would bring anyone to their knees, and this feeling was completely valid. As the tears stopped and the intensity of her anxiety and fear lessened, I reached back into my Calm Kit and had her move through the 5-4-3-2-1 Calming Technique for Anxiety. The method wasn't as playful as in the preschool classroom, but as we moved through the practice, it was just as effective. As she explored the final sensation of taste, I watched as she sat back in her chair, sighed deeply, and let it all settle. Over the next year we worked through a variety of mindfulness-based stress reduction techniques and saw both her personal and her professional life transform. Whenever we'd meet, we'd start our sessions in the same way, taking a deep breath in, breathing out, and letting it all settle.

Experiences like these two are why the phrase "let it set-tle" became my shorthand way to let people know it's OK to come back to yourself and settle into the moment. It's my small way of helping you as you work toward finding calm.

The Process of Letting It Settle

We'll cover many tools in this book as you start on the process of finding calm: mindfulness-based stress reduction practices, guided meditations, visualizations, somatic release exercises, and others. But here I want you to begin with the simplicity of finding your way back to the present moment and letting it settle with these four steps.

Step 1: Create a Space of Presence for Yourself

In those times of stress and anxiety, whatever they may be for you, it's important to remember to be gentle with yourself, just as you would with Jack. You would never judge him for having an intense reaction to a stressful situation, so why are you judging yourself for having an intense reaction to the stressful situation you're going through? That judgment isn't helpful, and it isn't necessary.

Step 2: Acknowledge and Validate the Emotional Experience

"*Why* does it—your reaction to a stressful situation; a thought, feeling, or action—make perfect sense?" You'll hear that question from me a lot in this book. When you are feeling stressed or overwhelmed, it's time to explore. Given everything that is happening around you and everything you've experienced in your life, think about why it makes perfect sense to be feeling the way you are. When you can begin to validate an emotional experience, you lessen the weight that judgment places on you and open yourself up to find your way through the situation.

Step 3: Ground Yourself in the Present Moment

Present moment awareness is about bringing your attention back to the immediate world around you and the experience you're having in each moment. In moments of chaos, our minds can race to the past or to the future, and emotional triggers can shift our bodies into overdrive. Grounding yourself in the present moment allows you to see things as they are and make conscious decisions about what is best for you. It also opens your eyes to the beauty that exists around you. Use the 5-4-3-2-1 Calming Technique for Anxiety as a starting point for this grounding.

Step 4: Letting It Settle

Magic happens when the body and mind begin to release fear and come back to the here and now. There's a physical release of the muscles, a letting go of tension and tightness, a settling of the mind as intense and overly protective thoughts begin to fade away, and a slowing of the breath as the heart returns to a slower pace, no longer pumping frantically to ensure survival. Let a sense of calm wash over you as you let everything settle.

Calm Kit Tool #1: 5-4-3-2-1 Calming Technique for Anxiety

The 5-4-3-2-1 Calming Technique is a simple mindfulness exercise designed to help manage anxiety and ground yourself in the present moment. Here's how it works:

1. **Identify five things you can see.** Take a moment to look around and consciously identify five things you can see in your immediate environment. These can be objects, colors, or any visual stimuli. By focusing on your surroundings, you shift your attention away from anxious thoughts and into the present moment.
2. **Acknowledge four things you can touch.** Pay attention to the sensation of touch and identify four things you can physically touch or feel. This could include the texture of your clothing, the surface of a table, or the feeling of the floor beneath your feet. Engaging your sense of touch helps to anchor you in the present and provides a sense of grounding.
3. **Notice three things you can hear.** Tune in to your auditory surroundings and identify three things you can

hear. This might be the sound of traffic outside, birds chirping, or the hum of appliances. Listening to the sounds around you can help move your focus away from anxious thoughts and into the present moment.

4. **Recognize two things you can smell.** Take a moment to notice any scents or smells in your environment and identify two of them. This could be the aroma of food cooking, the scent of flowers, or even the smell of your own body wash. Focusing on your sense of smell can further ground you in the present moment and promote relaxation.

5. **Acknowledge one thing you can taste.** Finally, become aware of your sense of taste and identify one thing you can taste. This might involve taking a sip of water, chewing a piece of gum, or simply noticing the lingering taste of your last meal. Bringing attention to your sense of taste can help to anchor you further in the present moment and provide a sense of calm.

The 5-4-3-2-1 Calming Technique is a helpful tool for managing anxiety by redirecting your focus away from anxious thoughts and into your immediate sensory experience. You can practice it virtually anywhere and anytime you feel the need to ground yourself and alleviate feelings of anxiety or being overwhelmed.

2 Easing Anxiety

A Gentle Reminder

There will be times when, despite your best efforts, no matter how many breaths you take, minutes you spend meditating, walks you take, or friends you talk to, the weight of your responsibilities will feel too heavy, and it will seem like you are fighting a losing battle against stress and anxiety. I want you to know when that happens, you are not failing. You are not a failure. It's just that in that moment, those feelings were stronger than the tools you have. You'll get stronger, and your tools will get sharper, but feeling overwhelmed in a stressful situation is *not* a sign of weakness. It's a sign that you're moving through life, just like the rest of us. So be gentle with yourself as you sharpen your tools and gain new ones. Know that sometimes the best thing you can do in the face of an anxious moment is allow it to be there without judgment or shame.

oments of unease and distress will visit you from time to time. They can sneak in throughout life unexpectedly, not just during times traditionally thought of as stressful, like major life transitions and catastrophes, but also when the mind is merely wandering and exploring past memories or hypothetical future situations. Often the cause of anxiety is not immediately recognizable, but the sensations are felt deeply. The stomach sinks; the breath and heart rate quicken as a surge of blood rushes to the brain. A feeling of distress sets in accompanied by a rush of stress hormones, which activate the sympathetic nervous system and create a fight-or-flight response. These moments can be short-lived experiences of heightened stress surrounding specific events or part of more serious long-term anxiety disorders, such as generalized anxiety disorder, panic disorder, or social anxiety disorder. In these anxiety disorders, anxiety may be present in the absence of a stressor, and medical intervention may be required to alleviate the symptoms.

Mindfulness plays an important role in facing anxiety as it allows you to come back to the present moment and begin to become aware of what exists in the here and now. It's an exercise of noting how the body feels, how the breath feels, letting the thoughts of past or future melt away, and eventually allowing a settling back into a space of comfort. Many mindfulness-based stress reduction techniques and tools can be beneficial, but it's important to remember that not every tool will work in every situation. There will be days when pausing for a breath will radically change your mood and ground you back into the present moment and other days when that same breath will have no impact at all. That's why building an arsenal of tools to help you find calm is important; you won't have to rely on a single mode of help, but you can cycle through options that work for you in the moment.

We've already begun the process of building this arsenal of tools with the 5-4-3-2-1 Calming Technique for Anxiety (Chapter 1). Here I take you through four more mindfulness-based tools and techniques that can help you begin to return to a space of calm, leaving the chaos behind.

Introducing Mindfulness

There was a time when I was one of those people who rolled their eyes at the mention of mindfulness. It seemed like a gimmicky buzzword that was attached to every LinkedIn article and inspirational Ted Talk, but never with meaning or substance. I had a limited knowledge of the term's origins, but I associated it with monks on a mountaintop somewhere far away and couldn't understand how their methods could be helpful in my busy life as a New Yorker.

As a side note, the origins and historical context of mindfulness are fascinating, and I highly recommend getting a deeper understanding by reviewing literature by some of the great teachers on the subject, such as Thích Nhất Hạnh, Jon Kabat-Zinn, Sharon Salzberg, or Tara Brach. In this book, we're going to focus solely on the techniques and practices associated with mindfulness and how they relate to emotional regulation, loving-kindness, and self-worth.

Although mindfulness did not appeal to me initially, I was fortunate enough to have teachers who allowed me to experience its benefits rather than explain them to me. I'm very much an experiential learner and need to feel the efficacy of something before buying into it. You can present me with every scientific study in the world, including the many that support the benefits of mindfulness, but without actively feeling the benefits myself, I'm hesitant to try something in my life. My teaching and coaching are also based in this experiential learning style, and my goal is to provide clients the opportunity to feel the benefits first and then follow up with research-backed materials.

Experiencing Mindfulness

It was in that yoga studio in Queens where I sat for a meditation session and began to feel the benefits of mindfulness for the first time. After taking off my shoes and walking over to the cushion, I sat with my legs crossed and let myself sink into the cushion. It had been a long day of commuting, teaching toddlers, and schlepping through the city, and my anxiety was quite high. It had been a struggle to drag myself to the studio for class that night, but I was committed to finding a way to help with the anxiety that had persisted for several months. Yuval, our amazing teacher and guide, started class by speaking about the benefits of mindfulness and how conscious awareness of the present moment can help us begin to move through life without being led by old habits or fears. We can start to discern the difference between what exists in reality and what is an instinctive reaction based on old, patterned behaviors and beliefs.

With closed eyes, she had us begin to focus on connecting to the breath. She drew our minds to the simplicity of the inhale and exhale, the rise and fall of the belly, and slowly added the phrase "I'm aware of my inhale, I'm aware of my exhale." My mind was still focused on the day, trying to shake off the feelings of anxiety that existed within, but by connecting with that phrase, I was able to redirect my attention away from those thoughts and center me back on my breath. As we continued, I noticed that those thoughts did not hold the intensity that they had at the beginning of class. They were still there, but I didn't feel the need to be connected to them.

As the thoughts began to settle in connection with the breath, Yuval had us move on to an awareness of the body. The instructions were not to judge anything as good or bad or attempt to change anything but simply to bring awareness to each part of the body and check in. Starting with the crown of the head, I could feel the headache that lingered from a long day in the classroom with the kids. We then moved onto the eyes, and I recognized the tension held there; then I felt into the tightness of my jaw from clenching all day. Recognizing this tension in just the first few moments of my Body Scan, all I wanted to do was move to fix it—to crack my neck, wiggle my jaw, and grab an Advil from my bag—but Yuval's gentle voice reminded us to stay connected to the sensation and remove judgment, so I kept moving along with her guidance. As we passed through the body, I continued to note those spaces of tension and tightness but also began to recognize the areas that felt relaxed. By the time we finally moved down to the feet, I realized that my mind was no longer connecting to the thoughts that had been present all day. The spaces where tension existed before felt at ease, and my breathing felt deeper and more relaxed. It was the first time in months that I felt comfort, my mind free from the anxiety that had plagued me.

The meditation concluded with drawing our awareness to the emotional experiences present for us. Yuval invited us to connect with what was coming up for us in that moment and, again, to remove judgment. In the stillness and silence of that moment as we held a hand to our hearts, I started to allow myself to feel into a sense of loss. A feeling of sadness was there beneath the anxiousness, and it wasn't until I began to allow myself simply to be in the moment that I could connect with it. Allowing for that feeling to be present without pushing it away was a foreign sensation and took me away from the "brave little soldier" (as discussed in the preface) I had attempted to be since I was a child.

As the meditation came to an end, I had so many questions to ask. I wanted to know how this all worked. Why was I able to release tension? Why was I able to find a space of calm and settle my swirling thoughts? Why was sadness there when the anxiousness faded away? How could I harness the superpower that I just was shown? Yuval's simple answer to my questions and those of the others was "Consistency and patience." Find ordinary moments in life to practice mindfulness so that you can begin to observe the world within you and around you and not allow yourself to be led by old habits and fears.

Implementing Mindfulness

Over the next few months, I practiced bringing mindfulness into my everyday life. I would practice staying in the moment while brushing my teeth, noting each step as I walked down the street, and finding a way to allow the feelings to be present in moments of stress. I brought this practice into my life in many ways, but during a particularly anxious moment, I truly started to feel and understand the powerful benefits of mindfulness.

I remember it as clearly as yesterday. It was an early Monday morning, and I was braving the crowds of New York City on my way to work. I stepped onto the Q train from Brooklyn to the Upper East Side. The trip usually took 45 minutes but ended up being much longer that day. The trains were always crowded, but I squeezed my way into a sea of commuters and grabbed a spot. I squished myself between a woman wearing a bulky winter coat and a middle schooler with an oversize backpack that he refused to take off, repeatedly bumping into me. The heat from all the people in winter garb made the temperature rise to what felt like 90 degrees. Finally we left the station. As we went through the tunnel and over the bridge, we made several more stops, each one adding more people, drawing me closer to those around me. At that point I could feel the heat continuing to rise and sweat beginning to pool on my forehead and lower back. My heart rate was getting a bit quicker, but I felt safe knowing that an end was in sight: In just three more stops I'd be able to get off and head to work.

After we left one of the stations, there was a loud *pop*, followed by the screeching of the train's wheels as we came to a complete stop. The conductor's muffled voice announced something inaudible, but incredibly loud. The usual moans and groans came from the passengers as we all prepared for the delay we knew was inevitable.

Each minute on a stalled train under the streets of New York feels like an hour, and the energy of the people around you, all starting to realize that they are going to be late to wherever they were headed and with no cell reception to alert anyone aboveground, adds to the frustration of the moment. As the minutes ticked by, as heat continued to rise, I was starting to hyperventilate and could feel a numbness in my hands and feet. I was beginning to go into a full sweat as my nervous system attempted to cool my body down. With sweat pouring down and my heart rate increasing, I was about to panic. When I had panicked before, I was not able to escape my mind thoughts; now I was physically trapped on a train underground.

Thirty minutes passed, and I was starting to gasp for air. I felt like I was desperately trying to yawn but couldn't get enough air to reach the point of relief. This shallow breathing continued, and with each breath, the inhale felt shorter and shorter. At this point, feeling that my lungs were not able to get enough air, my mind raced to seek safety. I urgently sought a window to break, a door to force open, or any space that would give me the air that I desperately needed. The kid's backpack continued to bump into me, reminding me that there was nowhere to move to; the car was too full to find safety. I started to prepare myself for the worst, and I felt myself slipping into a full panic attack.

In that moment, I suddenly remembered how calm I felt during that first meditation in the yoga studio and started to retrace the steps that I could remember. I drew my attention to my breath and felt its shallowness. Closing my eyes, I simply focused on the inhale and the exhale. I softly repeated the phrase "I'm aware of my inhale, I'm aware of my exhale." In that moment I recognized how panicked I was and how it was affecting my breath. Rather than try to fix it or change it, though, I continued to draw my attention to those words. Slowly I could feel each breath getting longer and deeper until that feeling of relief from a deep breath finally returned.

With my breath settled and my attention dropping away from the thoughts of panic, I started to connect with my body and scan from the crown of my head to my toes. I began to recognize the heat of my body and the dampness from the sweat on my forehead. There was a tightness in every muscle in my body and pain in my joints from standing stiffly for so long. Through it all, I simply allowed myself to become aware of the sensations. I noted the spaces of tension and acknowledged a momentary connection to a feeling of ease. I let that tension be there, and as I continued to connect to my breath, I felt an ease in my throat and then my chest and then I noticed a full release throughout my body.

Finally I drew my hand onto my heart, allowing myself to feel what was present underneath the physical manifestation of anxiety. I tapped into a sense of fear. In the confines of the subway car, my mind had been taking me to a place in which death was imminent. I was certain that the air was going to run out, that my heart would give up, and that I would fall to the ground and never rise. That deep-rooted fear was forcing me to prepare for the end and causing me to ignore reality and to focus solely on instinctive reactions. In giving myself permission to be with that fear, I was able to start to notice the spaces of safety that existed around me. I could speak gently to myself as I grounded myself back into the moment until the train jolted forward and began to move toward the next stop.

The situation didn't need to change for me to find calm. When my body, mind, and emotions began to settle, I was still sandwiched between the woman with the large winter coat and the kid with his backpack. Airflow hadn't magically returned, and the train hadn't started moving. I was in the exact same situation under the exact same circumstances, but my ability to connect mindfully had shifted. Mindfully drawing awareness and attention to my breath and body allowed me to recognize the present moment and see that while I was dealing with a great sense of discomfort and an unfortunate situation, I was not in the dire situation that my mind was making this out to be. Instead of being led by the reactions of fear that were causing heightened levels of anxiety, I was able to ground back into the reality of the moment and find the safety that existed on that train until I was able to exit and get aboveground.

The Process of Easing Anxiety

In those moments of anxiety, connecting mindfully to the present moment is a wonderful tool to start to find your way back to center. But as I learned at the beginning of my mindfulness journey, progress comes from consistency and patience. As you move through the anxiety that presents itself in your own life, remember to find ordinary moments to practice mindfulness so that you can begin to observe the world within you and around you and not allow yourself to be led by old habits and fears. And through it all, be patient and gentle with yourself.

The following steps will help you on your journey and can be part of a daily practice of meditation and mindfulness.

Step 1: Connect to the Breath

Begin to notice the breath as it enters and exits the body. A common phrase that can be attached to draw attention away from thoughts is: "I'm aware of my inhale, I'm aware of my exhale." Other options can be drawing awareness to the temperature of the breath on the inhale and exhale or observing the rise and fall of the belly on each breath.

Step 2: Draw Awareness to Thought

Allow yourself to become aware of thoughts that are entering at that moment. Avoid the urge to judge them as good or bad or to follow them. Simply note them as thoughts and make the conscious choice to redirect to either your breath or your body.

Step 3: Body Scan

Beginning at the crown of the head, bring awareness to each part of your body. It's important to allow yourself simply to note the sensations present, not labeling them as good or bad and not trying to fix the sensation in the moment. There may be a natural relaxing of the body as you move through the Body Scan, but there is no need to actively fix anything. Approach the Body Scan with a sense of curiosity, and note the spaces of tension and the spaces of ease.

Step 4: Connect to the Heart

Give yourself a moment to connect with the heart and begin to examine the emotional experience that is present for you. In moments of anxiety, most likely an underlying emotion is present. Once the body begins to release the tension held by anxiety, start to examine what it was blanketing. This can be fear, sadness, loss, or even excitement. Let yourself be with that emotion. From there make a conscious decision regarding what would best serve you and help you move through that emotion.

Step 5: Find the Spaces of Safety

Pause to recognize the safety surrounding you. Take in the reassuring sights, sounds, and sensations in your environment—the warmth of sunlight, the comforting aroma of familiar surroundings, or the gentle rhythm of nature. Shift your focus to the present moment, releasing concerns about the past or future. Allow yourself to fully experience the calm and relaxation these cues evoke within you. Embrace the sense of security they provide, reaffirming your resilience in the face of challenges. Trust in the inherent safety of the present moment, finding solace and comfort and a release from the grips of anxiety.

Calm Kit Tool #2: Body Scan

The Body Scan is a mindfulness practice that involves systematically bringing awareness to different parts of the body, usually starting from the top of the head and moving down to the toes. Here's how to do a Body Scan:

1. **Find a comfortable position.** Begin by finding a comfortable position to sit or lie down. You can close your eyes if it feels comfortable, but it's not necessary. Allow your body to relax and settle into a comfortable posture.
2. **Bring attention to the breath.** Take a few deep breaths to center yourself and bring your attention to the present moment. Notice the sensation of the breath as it enters and leaves your body, without trying to change it in any way. You can use the phrase "I'm aware of my inhale, I'm aware of my exhale" to maintain focus.
3. **Start at the top of the head.** Begin the Body Scan by bringing your awareness to the top of your head. Notice any sensations, tension, or feelings of warmth or coolness in this area. Take a moment to fully acknowledge and accept whatever sensations arise.
4. **Move down the body.** Slowly move your attention down through the body, one part at a time. You can move sequentially, starting with the forehead, then the eyes,

the cheeks, the jaw, and so on. Alternatively, you can choose to focus on specific areas of tension or discomfort.

5. **Notice sensations.** As you scan each part of the body, pay attention to any sensations you encounter, such as tingling, warmth, tightness, or relaxation. If you notice areas of tension or discomfort, simply observe them without judgment or the need to change them.

6. **End with the breath.** Once you have completed the Body Scan, take a few moments to return your attention to your breath. Notice how your body feels as a whole, and take a few deep breaths to recenter yourself before slowly opening your eyes, if they were closed.

The Body Scan is a powerful mindfulness practice that can help to reduce stress, promote relaxation, and increase body awareness. It can be done as a stand-alone practice or as part of a longer meditation session. Regular practice can help to cultivate a greater sense of presence and connection with the body, leading to an increased overall sense of well-being.

3 Facing Fear

Gentle Reminder

As you get closer to obtaining or achieving the things that are meaningful and important to you, a certain level of fear will arise. And at times that fear will become so overwhelming that you will want to stop before you take the next step, to rush back to safety and wait until the fear subsides. But in doing so, you might be waiting around for a long time. The truth about fear is that it rarely disappears with time; rather, it disappears when it is challenged by your resilience in the face of it. Recognizing that fear is there, allowing it to be there, and then making the conscious choice to step forward in the face of that fear isn't easy and won't feel good. But what you've been waiting for lies on the other side of that fear.

The protective nature of the human body and the lengths it will go to keep us safe has always fascinated me. Signals, signs, and warnings are constantly firing as we move throughout our day to keep us safe and well. These signals are prompts from our nervous system that it is time to go into action and fight against perceived threats or run away from dangers we are sensing. I like to think of our sympathetic nervous system as a protective parent on a mission to save us from the world we're living in. It constantly scans the playground and makes sure we don't fall from the monkey bars, scrape our knees, or get our feelings hurt by bullies. With each bump and bruise, our sympathetic nervous system becomes more aware of potential dangers and leaps into action in anticipation. But just as an overprotective parent often keeps children from growth opportunities and leaves them ill-prepared for real-life situations, so too can our overprotective nervous system, especially when it begins to sense a threat and push us into a space of fear.

In moments of fear, the body and mind begin to react in ways to move us away from perceived threats in the quickest way possible. The body begins to alert us of danger through a series of physical manifestations: the racing heart, the sweating palms, the hot flushing of the body. All of these physical manifestations are accompanied by swirling thoughts telling us that we should be prepared to take action to move us back to safety quickly, even when the experience at hand actually may bring us growth or opportunity. Although fear may be justified in certain situations, often it's simply a reaction to a situation too close to a past hardship or to an undesired future and ignores the truth of the present. In those moments of fear when you feel that overprotective parent yelling at you to get off the slide before you hurt yourself, it's important to stop, come back to the present, and determine if that voice is worth listening to or if you should just say "Thank you for trying to protect me, but let's work together to find a space of calm so I can decide if this is an opportunity I want to take."

Honing in on Your Fears

It was 2 am on a Monday, and while I should have been sleeping, I was scrolling through my phone in an apparent attempt to reach the end of the internet, which felt more easier to do than getting the rest I needed. While swiping through posts on social media, my phone started to buzz, and Caleb's name popped up. It was rare to get a text at that time from Caleb, but a phone call was alarming. I answered and immediately could hear quick, stuttered speech and labored breathing on the other end of the phone. Trying to figure out what was wrong, I asked him to slow down and give me a quick rundown of what was going on. Was he OK? Was he in danger? Did he need help?

Caleb was an incredibly bright student whom I had the pleasure of coaching throughout his senior year at New York University. His therapist had recommended he start to work on bringing mindfulness and meditation into his life to help with school-related stress, so I was brought in to help. Throughout our time together, we worked to find ways for him to use the tenets of mindfulness to find a space of calm during the busyness of his senior year. His meditation practice became an important part of his routine, and he was able to find a balance between his perfectionist tendencies that led him to overwork and miss out on his social life and the enjoyment of his final year with his friends.

During our last session, Caleb had opened up about his recent acceptance letter to Yale grad school and his parents' excitement when he had told them. His mother had already alerted the family group text, and messages of congrats were flooding in. It was what they had dreamed of for him since he was little: graduating with honors and heading off to Yale to pursue his master's. I could sense Caleb's understandable feeling of being overwhelmed as he talked about it. There was a lot of pressure being the "golden boy" of the family, and we worked through ways to plan for inevitable stress as he headed into a huge shift in his life.

I knew that, given everything going on in his life, there would be challenges as graduation came closer, but as I listened to him try to form the words to express what was happening for him, I knew that he was trapped in fear. That protective part of him was trying to prevent him from moving forward, and he didn't yet have the tools to recognize what was happening.

Eventually I was able to start walking him through a process of mindfully approaching fear. We began recognizing what was going on for him. What feelings were there? Where was the fear showing up in his body? The goal was for him to get out of his thinking mind for a moment and direct his attention back to the physical and emotional experience. He was able to start to express that, in that moment, he felt a tightening of his throat, a constricting of his chest, a racing heart, and his entire body felt flush with heat. He felt anxious, nervous, a sense of dread, and beneath all of that was fear. The act of stating that he was feeling fear allowed him to begin to recognize what was happening and let it be there.

Next we started to explore the thoughts that were present for him. They were coming in so fast and ranged from a hyperfocus on his body and concern for his physical safety to the replaying of past memories, thinking about times he felt embarrassed and filled with regret. But the thought that continued to spiral the loudest was that he wasn't going to be able to make it at Yale. His mind was trying to convince him that he had been fooling everyone by trying to appear smarter than he actually was and that, surrounded by brilliant minds, he would be seen as a fraud and disappoint his family.

When examining his thoughts, we identified the source of the fear: He thought he was not good enough. With all of the attention and expectations placed on him, he would fail, and the world would finally see that his deepest fear was a reality. When Caleb was able to say those words out loud and identify where this feeling was coming from, he almost sighed with relief. Recognizing that all of the signals and reactions his body and mind were experiencing were connected to this fear brought a sense of peace.

From an outside perspective, it would be easy to say this was a wildly irrational thought and he had nothing to be afraid of. His track record at school was stellar, and he was consistently praised for his hard work and talents. But to Caleb, this deep-seated fear had been with him for years. He had pushed it aside and buried it, but it had always been with him.

In working toward acceptance and nonjudgment, I pulled out my favorite question: "*Why does it make perfect sense?*" In this case, "it" refers to the intense emotional reaction he had experienced that night. Why did it make perfect sense that, given everything he had experienced in his life and everything going on, he would have such an intense reaction of fear? With that question, Caleb was able to start to speak about the pressure he was under, the expectations he placed on himself, the fact that his family's approval meant everything to him, and the thought of letting them down was crushing. He recognized that Yale had not only been their dream for him, but it really was his dream. It was meaningful and important, and the fear of losing out on the opportunity was too much to handle. When he started to see things from that perspective, he was able to feel a sense of empathy for himself, to remove the judgment, and to fully accept that it made sense that he'd be reacting this way.

Implementing Somatic Therapies

As Caleb started to settle into his fear, we returned to the body through somatic work to help him find his way back to a regulated nervous system. The word "somatic" refers to the integration of the mind and body, emphasizing the connection between physical sensations, movements, and emotional experiences. Somatic therapies help to connect the brain and body through touch and movement. Such therapies include exercising your nervous system and getting used to bodily sensations and cues from your body in a way that you don't have to fear them anymore.

To find that space of safety, I invited Caleb to interlace his thumbs and cross his arms over his chest with the tip of the middle finger from each hand directly below the opposite collarbone. This pose creates the appearance of a butterfly resting on the chest. As he closed his eyes, I invited him to connect to his breath and slowly begin to tap on his chest with alternate hands, emulating the beating of a butterfly's wings. With slow and consistent tapping moving from side to side and mindfully breathing, Caleb started to release the tension from his shoulders, his body started to loosen, the heat he felt in his body dropped, and his racing heart began to slow. In that moment of settling, he returned to a regulated nervous system and was ready to start to look at that fear again.

As his body and mind began to settle, I asked Caleb to think of the spaces of safety that existed in this situation. If the fear was that he would not be enough and would fail, what were the items that kept him safe from that? What things did he have in place to prevent that, and what were things would protect him even if that failure were to come true?

Caleb recognized his own ability to excel in academic settings. Graduating from New York University with honors was hardly an easy feat, so he used that as a reference point to present in the face of fear. He recognized that his family had always been there for him and that, although they expected a lot from him, in moments when he really needed them, they were there and would continue to be. Then he spoke of the safety of knowing how to return to center in moments of stress. He had proved last semester that, even when things were hard and he felt an incredible amount of stress and pressure, he could return home to himself and find his way through it. All of these spaces of safety already existed, but in the intensity of his current fear, he was blind to them. Drawing light on them helped him to feel strong enough to move forward and safe enough to keep going.

Finally we spoke about what he wanted to do in the face of that fear. From this settled space, did it make sense for him to change course and listen to the overly protective fear-based response, or would he be able to make the conscious choice to move forward in the face of fear? The answer was clear for him. Although that fear would pop up over the next few months, he was able to walk through this process each time and find his way back to the courage to take the next step forward.

Before the call wrapped up, I asked Caleb how he could take that first step forward. What could he do to ensure that he was able to face his fear and prove to himself that, even with fear present, he could continue to be in motion? It wouldn't be the larger action points of announcing his acceptance to his professors and friends; that seemed too scary, and at this point, at least, would push him further into the fear. But what he could do was to sign the acceptance letter and make a declaration to himself that this move was right for him and real. It felt like a push but not a shove, and it was something that made him face that fear and choose to move forward toward his dreams.

Fear versus Denial

So often we hear that we need to "crush fear." Fearlessness is placed on a high pedestal, and we're told that to be a self-actualized human, we cannot allow fear to be present in our lives. We're told to judge ourselves poorly when we do feel fear. But the absence of fear in a situation that warrants some level of fear isn't fearlessness; it's denial. As humans, we always will feel a level of fear. By pretending that it doesn't exist and forcing our way through life ignoring it, we're ignoring the beauty of our body's protective mechanism and bypassing learning experiences that can help us approach similar situations in the future.

It's not that we want to be fearless. It's that we want to be resilient in the face of fear and utilize fear to better understand ourselves and gain control over our initial responses to stressful situations. Learning to sit with fear and allow it to be present gives us the ability to connect with ourselves and gain insight into how and why we react to the world around us. With that awareness, we gain the ability to choose how to move forward. Instead of blindly reacting based on past experiences, we're making the conscious choice to move through fear, trusting that what is on the other side is worth the momentary discomfort of sitting with the emotion.

The Process of Facing Fear

Moving through fear isn't exactly a natural response, and doing so will take time, patience, and the right tools. Let's revisit the steps that Caleb went through on that fearful night and see if you can implement them into your life the next time fear pops up for you.

Step 1: Recognize and Acknowledge Your Fear

At times we try to suppress or ignore our fear, leaning into that space of denial, but that only makes the fear more powerful. Instead, gently bring your awareness to the fear you're experiencing. Allow it to be there, and note how it's showing up for you without trying to push it away or run from it.

Step 2: Observe Your Thoughts

As fear arises, observe your thoughts without judgment. Your mind may create worst-case scenarios or irrational beliefs. Recognize these thoughts as mental constructs and gently redirect your focus to the present.

Step 3: Identify the Source

Try to identify the source of your fear. Is it related to a specific event, a past trauma, or an imagined future scenario? Understanding the root cause of your fear can help you address it more effectively.

Step 4: Acceptance and Nonjudgment

Practice self-compassion and self-acceptance. Understand that fear is a natural human response to perceived threats or uncertainties. Avoid self-judgment, and remember that feeling fear doesn't make you weak or inadequate; it makes you human.

Step 5: Calming Techniques

Use mindfulness or somatic techniques and tools like Deep Breathing, or a Body Scan, or grounding exercises like the Butterfly Hug to stay present with your fear. The goal is to begin to calm your nervous system and bring your attention back to the present.

Step 6: Note the Spaces of Safety That Exist Around You

To return to that space of calm, take yourself out of your thinking mind, which is alerting you to the threat associated with the fear, and find the spaces that exist that will be there as you move through the fear.

Step 7: Make a Conscious Decision

From these spaces, start to begin to identify your options. First carefully identify what those impulses to action are.

What is your body and mind telling you needs to happen for you to be safe? What are those impulses? And then recognize that an impulse is just an option, not a necessity. Look further and decide what other choices may be present for you and most align with what you want for your life. Then, from a calm and centered space, make the choice that best serves you in that moment. This choice will be the first step that will lead you toward where you ultimately want to be.

Calm Kit Tool #3: Butterfly Hug

The Butterfly Hug is a somatic exercise used in therapeutic settings, particularly in the treatment of trauma and stress. Here's an explanation of how to do the Butterfly Hug exercise.

1. **Find a comfortable position.** Begin by finding a comfortable seated or standing position. You can also do this exercise lying down if that feels more comfortable for you. Close your eyes if you prefer, but it's not necessary.
2. **Cross your arms.** Interlace your thumbs and cross your arms over your chest with the tip of the middle finger from each hand directly below the opposite collarbone.
3. **Tap alternately.** Using a gentle tapping motion, alternately tap your hands on your shoulders. As you tap, imagine you're creating a rhythm similar to the fluttering of butterfly wings. The taps should be light and rhythmic, with a comfortable intensity.
4. **Focus on breathing.** As you continue the tapping motion, focus on your breath. Take slow, deep breaths in through your nose and out through your mouth. Allow your breath to be smooth and steady, without forcing it in any way.

5. **Bring attention to sensations.** While tapping and breathing, bring your attention to any sensations you experience in your body. Notice the feeling of your hands tapping on your shoulders, the rhythm of your breath, and any other sensations that arise.

6. **Stay present.** If your mind starts to wander or you notice yourself becoming distracted, gently bring your focus back to the present moment. Use the tapping and breathing as anchors to keep you grounded in the here and now.

7. **Continue for several minutes.** Practice the Butterfly Hug exercise for several minutes, or for as long as feels comfortable for you. You can experiment with different tapping rhythms and speeds to see what feels most soothing and calming for you.

8. **Reflect.** After you've completed the exercise, take a moment to reflect on how you feel. Notice any changes in your body, emotions, or mental state. You may feel more relaxed, centered, or grounded after practicing Butterfly Hug.

The Butterfly Hug exercise is a simple yet powerful somatic technique that can help to regulate emotions, reduce anxiety, and promote a sense of calm and safety. It can be used as a self-soothing tool in moments of distress or as part of a regular self-care routine.

4

Meditations and Daily Habits for Finding Calm

This chapter provides a set of meditative practices and daily habits that you can incorporate into your life as you work toward finding calm. You can return to the meditations in times of need or practice them daily. By embracing the simplicity of these practices and committing to consistent habits, you can gradually unlock the transformative power of calm in your life. Whether you're seeking relief from stress and anxiety or simply striving to live more fully in the present moment, these tools will support you on your journey toward greater well-being and fulfillment.

Meditations for Finding Calm

The following three meditations offer distinct pathways to finding calm. The Body Scan Meditation guides you through a systematic exploration of bodily sensations, fostering present-moment awareness and the release of tension. The Four-Point Breathing Meditation regulates the breath, activating the body's relaxation response and grounding the mind in the rhythm of inhales and exhales. The Safe Space Meditation provides a mental refuge, allowing you to immerse yourself in a tranquil environment, triggering the brain's relaxation mechanisms. Each practice cultivates mindfulness, reduces stress, and promotes a sense of inner peace, offering diverse tools to navigate the complexities of daily life with greater calmness and resilience.

Body Scan Meditation

The Body Scan Meditation guides you through a systematic exploration of your body, from your toes through the crown of your head, bringing awareness to each part and noticing any sensations without judgment. This practice helps you develop mindfulness of your body, allowing you to release tension and stress stored in your muscles and tissues. Regular practice of the Body Scan Meditation can reduce anxiety, improve sleep quality, and enhance overall well-being. By cultivating awareness of your body, you can learn to respond to physical sensations with compassion and care, which promotes greater relaxation and a sense of calm.

Start by finding the most comfortable sitting position that you can. Allow your lower half to root down into what's beneath you. If it feels right and safe to do so, close your eyes or focus your eyes softly gazing downward.

Now draw your awareness to your breath. Feel the inhale and the exhale, and note how the air enters in through the nostrils and out through the mouth. With each breath allow your body to settle, to sink, into the cushion or chair.

Begin to bring attention to your feet. Note the toes, the heels, the soles of your feet. Without needing to fix or change anything, become aware of the sensations in the feet, noting if there's any tension or tightness. Then draw your awareness to your ankles, up through your shins and your calves, into your knees. Begin to note the sensations in the upper legs through the quadriceps and hamstrings. Connect the awareness to the seat, the hips, the pelvis, and allow the entire lower body to sink—not needing to hold on but letting everything feel heavy and loose.

Connect with the sensations in your lower back wrapping around into the stomach. Let go of the need to hold on, and feel everything relax. Draw that awareness up through the back into the shoulders. Allow the shoulders to drop as you check in with your arms, elbows, forearms, wrists, and into the hands through each finger.

Now draw the awareness into the chest. Feel into the muscles of the chest, and feel the rise and fall with each inhale and exhale. Begin to feel into the neck and up into the throat. With a sense of curiosity, begin to explore the roof of your mouth, teeth, tongue, lips. Notice the jaw and allow it to loosen.

(continued)

Let yourself become aware of the sensations in the face: eyes, ears, nose, mouth, and onto the forehead to the space between your eyes. Take that attention and awareness into the crown of your head, and then scan down through the body and note any places of tension or tightness or anywhere that might be calling out for your attention.

Connect the breath to that space of tension and feel the inhale, allow it to expand and return on the exhale, and let it go. Once again feel the inhale connecting with that space of tension and tightness, and let it go. Allow the entire body to relax and continue to sink deeper and deeper into what's beneath you.

Give yourself permission to feel into a sense of calm within the body. When it feels right, begin to awaken your fingers and toes, become aware of your senses, the sounds within the room, the smells. Then bring your hands together in front of you, rubbing them together and feeling into the sensation of touch.

When it feels right and safe to do so, flutter your eyes open. Take in the space around you and enter back, feeling connected and calm.

Four-Point Breathing Meditation

The Four-Point Breathing Meditation is an exploration of mindfulness and self-awareness that draws your focus to four key points connected to the breath: nose, chest, stomach, and edges of the body. During the meditation, you become attuned to the sensations of each breath cycle, from the cool air entering your nostrils to the rise and fall of your chest and the expansion and contraction of your stomach. With each inhale and exhale, you deepen your connection with the present moment, allowing you to take up space and feel grounded in your physical presence. This practice heightens mindful awareness of breath and provides a sense of calm and centeredness.

Find a comfortable position, seated or lying down. Let your entire body feel a sense of comfort and stillness as you draw a deep breath in through the nose and breathe out through the mouth, letting it all settle. As you allow the mind to relax, the body to soften, and the emotions to be present without judgment, either close your eyes or maintain a soft focus with your eyes softly gazing downward.

Start to connect to your breath and become aware of the inhale entering in through the nose and out through the mouth. As you explore this breath, note the temperature of the air as it enters in through the nostrils and the difference in temperature as the air exits through the mouth. Breathe in and breathe out. [Repeat three times.] Next become aware of the breath entering the chest. Allow your chest to rise with each inhale and to

(continued)

fall with each exhale. Begin to note the sensations in the chest as the breath enters and exits. [Repeat three times.]

Next become aware of the stomach. Begin to draw the air into your belly. Feel the inhale creating an expansion of the belly outward, and feel the stomach return to a place of stillness as you exhale. Take three breath cycles to feel into the expansion and settling of the belly. [Repeat three times.]

For the final point of connection, note the edges of the body that separates you from the openness of space around you. Then note the space in front of you; the space to either side of you; the space behind you, above you, and below you. Allow the breath to press the edges of the body into the openness of space with each inhale and give yourself permission to take up space and become as large as you would like to. With each exhale, return to center. Move through three cycles of this expansive breath and feel the body move like a wave rushing in and rolling out as you breathe in and breathe out. [Repeat three times.]

Bring the breath back to its typical pattern and begin to become aware of the present moment. Begin to move your hands and feet to awaken them, and move any part of your body that feels tense or tight. When it feels right and it's safe to do so, flutter your eyes open. Take in the space around you, and enter back connected and calm.

Safe Space Meditation

The Safe Space Meditation is designed specifically to help you find inner comfort and security during moments of stress and anxiety. By guiding you through a series of visualizations, this meditation encourages you to imagine yourself in a serene environment, ultimately leading you to discover a personal safe space where you can experience the familiar feelings of warmth and tranquility that exist in a real or imagined setting of your choice. Visualization is a crucial aspect of this practice, as it empowers you to create a mental sanctuary where you can seek refuge from fear and anxiety. This visualization technique not only cultivates a sense of calmness but also enhances your mindfulness and emotion-regulation skills. The ability to find a safe space within yourself is a valuable tool for managing stress and anxiety, promoting your mental well-being, and fostering resilience in challenging situations.

Begin to find a space of comfort, either seated or lying down. Let your body settle into a space where it can be still and without distraction, allowing your mind to wander. Now bring to mind a place that reminds you of safety and comfort. It can be an imagined place or the image of a specific place in your life. The visualization should be detailed enough so that you can imagine specific details and comforting enough to provide a sense of calm and safety.

Start by connecting to your breath. Feel the inhale through your nose and the exhale through your

(continued)

mouth with each breath. If it feels right and safe to do so, go ahead and close your eyes or keep a soft focus gazing downward. Allow the body to settle. Allow the mind to settle. Allow any stirring emotions to settle and, with that settling, begin to draw your awareness to your imagination.

Imagine that you are walking down a path in the woods. Hear the crunch of the leaves beneath your feet, feel the rush of the wind as the breeze comes through the trees and past you, and see the tall oak trees that line your path with their branches letting small streams of light through the canopy of leaves above. Continue walking down this path, allowing yourself to imagine all of your senses exploring these woods. Imagine painting in the picture of your surroundings in your mind. [Allow about 2 minutes for this part of the exercise.]

As you continue to walk down the path, you glimpse a large body of water ahead. On the edge of the water is a wooden rowboat. It seems to be waiting for you. As you climb into the boat, you feel the rocking of the water beneath you.

Grab the oars and begin to row. The smooth water is guiding you toward an island in the distance. As you get closer and closer, you begin to recognize something on the island. With five simple strokes of the oars, you arrive at the dock: 5-4-3-2-1.

You step off the boat onto a beautiful island with the warm sun shining on you. As you walk away from the dock, you see a blue door in the distance and feel drawn to explore. There's a familiar feeling to the door, but you're not sure why. As you approach the door, you reach an arm out to open it. As it swings open, you recognize your safe space behind that door, the space where you feel most comfortable and calm.

Step into the space and feel the warmth and comfort; it's like coming home. Sit for a few moments and connect with what it feels like to be here. Note your emotional connection to this calming and safe environment. [Allow as much time as necessary, typically 3 to 5 minutes, to be in your safe space.]

After a few minutes, you are feeling safe and comfortable. Recognize that it's time to leave before the sun goes down. Say good-bye to anyone who may have been there with you and walk back out the door.

And as you step out the door, you realize that you are back in the present moment. You are still holding on to that sense of safety and calm but are connected to your current space. From this space of safety, begin to notice the sounds within the room, the smells. Note your sense of taste and touch. Bring your hands together in front of you to experience touch. And then finally, when it feels right and safe to do so, flutter your eyes open and connect with your sense of sight. Fully return to the space and experience it while holding on to that safety and comfort of your safe space.

Place a hand on your heart and realize that you can always return to that space and always find safety within. Take a deep breath in, breathe out, and let it all settle.

Daily Habits for Finding Calm

Incorporate these three daily habits into your routine to help take you back to mindfulness and calm.

Daily Practice of Mindful Awareness

Cultivate a daily practice of mindful awareness, where you intentionally bring your attention to the present moment without judgment. Doing so can involve formal meditation practices, such as the Four-Point Breathing Meditation or the Body Scan Meditation, or informal practices, such as mindful walking or eating, where you simply bring your full attention to the experience of common tasks that often are done without thought or attention. By regularly tuning in to your present experience, you can develop greater awareness and acceptance of whatever arises, which fosters a sense of inner peace and calm.

Daily Mindfulness Breaks

Incorporate periods of mindfulness throughout your day to pause, breathe, and reconnect with the present moment. Doing this could be as simple as taking a few deep breaths before starting a task, practicing mindful eating during meals, or taking a brief walk outside to appreciate nature. Setting a calendar invite for a "Mindful Moment" throughout the day is a great way to reserve time to practice grounding yourself back into the present moment. These mindfulness breaks can help you navigate stressors with greater ease and maintain a sense of calm amid daily challenges.

Daily Stress Reduction Techniques

Integrate stress reduction techniques into your daily routine to help manage the inevitable challenges of life. To promote relaxation and alleviate tension in the body and mind, include deep breathing exercises, such as the Four-Point Breathing Meditation; grounding exercises, such as the 5-4-3-2-1 Calming Technique for Anxiety (Chapter 1); the Body Scan (Chapter 2); somatic practices like the Butterfly Hug (Chapter 3); or guided imagery, like the Safe Space Meditation described earlier in this chapter. By proactively engaging in these practices, you can build resilience and cultivate a greater sense of calm in the face of stressors.

PART 2

Coming Home to Yourself

5

Gentle Reminder

Not all of the thoughts that enter your mind are worth listening to. Sometimes completely nonsensical notions will race across your mind, but just because a thought is there does not make it true. At times you will experience automatic responses of negativity to stimuli around you. Unless these automatic responses are serving you in some way, you can discard them immediately. You can choose to step back and listen to these thoughts, assess their value, and allow them to pass if they don't serve you, just as you would with advice from a friend.

Begin to cultivate awareness of your thoughts by observing them without judgment. Take a moment to consider whether each thought aligns with your values and aspirations or if it pulls you further away from your desired path. If a thought doesn't serve your well-being, gently let it go and return home to yourself.

used to pray every night that I would wake up as someone else. It was a prayer of longing to be someone who was less sensitive, less shy, who was more athletic, smarter, someone whose family wasn't broken and didn't have to hide so much of who he was from the world to feel safe. But each day I would wake up and look in the mirror and still see the reflection of someone I didn't want to be. I could point out every flaw that existed within me but was incapable of seeing the good, even when others pointed that good out to me. From the outside, I was a golden boy who was thriving despite difficult circumstances at home. I was kind and polite and knew from an early age how to make others feel comfortable, even when I wasn't. But beneath all of that was a deep discomfort and desire for change.

Over time, those unanswered prayers turned to action as I started to craft an idealized version of myself. This version was someone I felt would be worthy of love and didn't possess my imperfections. I tried to change everything about myself to be that person, including how I looked, how I acted, and whom I interacted with. Each new accomplishment distracted me from the pain I was feeling and, for a moment, took focus away from the parts of me I was ashamed of.

To some extent, this method worked. There were moments of happiness and times when I could be proud of myself for my accomplishments, but all that pride in myself was based on external validation. I was allowing others to see only the parts of me that I felt were acceptable, and I was hiding all the rest. Eventually this pursuit of perfection became exhausting. No matter what I achieved, self-hatred still existed within me, and I was unable to feel a sense of love. With every success, a voice within would get louder, telling me that I didn't deserve the win. With every new relationship, a reminder that I would never be worthy of love would ring in my ears. I was constantly rewriting my story when the old narrative no longer served me, writing a new chapter while running from people who knew the prior version of me, and creating a new main character while slowly losing essence of the person I truly was. That "brave little soldier" (discussed in the preface) marched forward, and I lost sight of the sensitive boy I once was.

With each new chapter of my life, I inevitably grew deeply unsettled and unable to feel at ease in my body or in my surroundings. Eventually I couldn't run any more. The pain associated with my anxiety led me to find a space of stillness and begin to listen to myself for the first time. I wasn't listening to the negative voices or the fear that forced me into action; I was listening to that still, small voice of knowing that comes in moments of silence. And as I got still, that voice began to remind me, quietly but fiercely, that it was time to go home.

Listening in the Stillness

The journey home to myself started from clearing away the noise and allowing myself to truly hear. My mind was always running, and only rarely did I stop moving long enough to be aware of my thoughts. In fact, it wasn't until I started studying mindfulness that I realized that I could observe my thoughts. Prior to that understanding, my thoughts dictated my actions. I was sure that if a thought was there, it must be worth listening to. And that included those self-deprecating and negative thoughts that kept me running from myself for so long.

But as I started to step back and become more interested in the awareness of my thoughts than I was with the thoughts themself, I came to realize that many were simply *not* worth listening to. And as I started getting more curious about the awareness of thought, I started to recognize that thoughts fell into a few different categories.

- **Catastrophizing thoughts** had me building what ifs and worst-case scenarios that allowed me to play out every possible negative outcome to a situation and caused me a great deal of stress and sleepless nights.
- **Rehearsing thoughts** had me continuously planning for future events and making sure that I was prepared for anything that might come my way.
- **Rehashing thoughts** replayed past events in my mind, furiously trying to find a reason or solution for what went wrong or shaming or embarrassing me for any imperfect action.
- **Gremlin thoughts** popped up to remind me that I was not good enough, or smart enough, or capable enough to do what was in front of me. These thoughts constantly pulled me back, berated me for any wrong action, and warned me of what could happen if I tried to go beyond the boundaries of where it felt safe.

When I started to recognize these patterns of thought and realize that most were fear based and protective in nature, my approach to life subtly shifted. Instead of instinctively acting on every thought, I started to challenge the thoughts and really consider if they were worth listening to. When I started to catastrophize, I was able to stop and challenge the thought with a simple question: What if it went well? This shifted my focus from the worst-case scenario to the best-case one. Neither of these thoughts was based in reality, but one left me sleepless and the other filled me with hope. When the rehearsing or rehashing thoughts came, I would draw myself back to the present moment, gently reminding myself that all that exists is right here in the present and that fretting or fearing things that don't exist only causes pain. It was a game of choice, and that choice was possible only with awareness of thought.

There was, however, one thought pattern that I couldn't quite shake.

Battling the Gremlin Thoughts

No matter how aware I was of the thinking mind or how much I tried to sit in the observer's seat, that pesky gremlin's incessant monologue convinced me every time that it was correct. It would tell me that I wasn't good enough to try something, and I would agree and avoid it entirely. It would point out my flaws and weaknesses, reminding me to hide myself from the world, and I would cover up those areas and hide away. That voice was holding me back from so many of the things that I was passionate about. It had kept me from pursuing career opportunities in the theater, kept me distant in relationships, and forced me to pursue only things that felt safe and easy, leading me in directions that felt inauthentic and misaligned. It also left me incapable of seeing the good that existed within me. But the voice had been around for so long that even when I practiced Mindful Awareness of Thought, I couldn't help but let it lead the way.

In Michael Singer's book *The Untethered Soul*, he describes this incessant inner monologue as your "inner roommate."

This is the most troubled, irritating, and emotionally reactive person who just happens to be shacked up in your house with you and never leaves. It's a voice that can pull you away from anything worthwhile and distract you at any time.

As I read *The Untethered Soul*, I started to get a deeper understanding of what I was dealing with and its impact on my life. One of the exercises that Singer suggested was to personify the inner roommate as someone beyond yourself, then start to listen carefully for the messages that are coming from that roommate and recognize how you react to them.

I sat and allowed myself to connect with my own inner roommate. Initially it wasn't pleasant. I pictured him as an intense and gruff man who was constantly yelling, and I felt fearful when he came into my mind's eye. When dealing with fear with our preschool students, one things we'd often do was to create a caricature of the fear so it wouldn't be so scary. The monster hiding in the dark wouldn't incite as much fear if you pictured him with silly glasses and three big toes. So, instead of looking at my inner roommate as a person I was fearful of, I wanted to create a silly monster of sorts that I could visualize and laugh at. The best way to stop fearing the proverbial monster under the bed is to picture him as a goofy and harmless oaf of a monster that just happened to get stuck there and probably could use your help getting out.

That contentious voice in my head soon became Magnor, a 600-pound green and white fluffy monster who wandered into the basement one day and, because his diet consisted only of Cheetos and Twinkies, got a bit too chubby to leave, so he stayed. Over the years he watched everything I did, tagging along everywhere from T-ball games to senior prom and sticking around through college and beyond. He had a front-row seat to every moment of my life: He watched me embarrass myself by stumbling over my words in front of my second-grade class; he saw me when my heart had been broken, when I was laughed at for crying in the gym, when I lost friends and loved ones and found out what it felt like to be left by those closest to me. From his space in the basement, Magnor watched it all. And as the years went by, he started to get quite protective of his buddy who lived upstairs. Having this intimate view into my feelings and thoughts, he could tell what hurt me the most and would send off warning signs if he thought I was getting too close to something that could create pain. And when he didn't feel like I was listening, those warning signs turned into shouts. Magnor knew exactly what it would take to stop me in my tracks, and he was willing to do whatever it took to make sure I was safe from what he perceived as threats. He'd use a series of phrases to warn me to be careful, to remind me of what happened last time something like this came up, and to ensure that I took a step back and kept us both safe and sound. His favorite was to tell me that I wasn't good enough or smart enough or capable of doing what I was trying to do, so I might as well not try. Most of the time, his tricks were effective and kept me safe but stuck.

Even though I couldn't see Magnor, in those moments of perceived threats, I could still hear his shouts. But as I grew older, his voice started to sound a lot like mine and those shouts quickly became my thoughts. Unable to separate myself from those thoughts, I came to believe that they were true. I wasn't good enough, I wasn't smart enough, I wasn't capable, so I came to believe that I should just not try.

I carried those beliefs around with me for years, not knowing that they were simple cries from a fluffy monster trying to keep me safe. I beat myself up and criticized everything about myself, holding on to those words as truth. I was inherently not good enough, and even if I did succeed, I was simply fooling everyone. One day I'd be found out.

Clearing the Noise

When I started to come home to myself and gain an understanding that I was the one observing the thoughts, I peeked down into the basement and saw that Magnor was still there. There he sat, shouting to protect me and feeling satisfied that he had done so for so long. We had a heart-to-heart one day, and I let him know that while I appreciated all these years of him trying to keep me from having to relive painful moments, I was fully capable of caring for myself. Now his methods were actually hurting me more than simply facing the life we were both afraid of.

Magnor wasn't ready to leave right then, but we made a plan to let him show up from time to time with gentler words of warning and the understanding that I wouldn't always listen to him. I would hear the shouts and make the choice that was best for me.

And with that agreement between us in place, the noise began to clear. Having this silly reference point to turn to in moments when my mind started to spew nonsense of inadequacy at me was incredibly helpful. It removed a heavy weight and gave me the ability to make a conscious choice in the face of fear. Those gremlin thoughts became warning signs instead of stop signs, and the ability to pause and make a choice that best served me gave me a sense of power over my own life. This strategy helped me begin to come home to myself.

Cultivating an Awareness of Thought

It's not uncommon to be deeply entwined with our thoughts and struggling to untangle them from our sense of self. It's important to remember that *our thoughts do not define us*. In other words, our thoughts are not us. One of my favorite metaphors to help demonstrate how thoughts work is to imagine your mind as a busy marketplace, buzzing with activity. Thoughts are like vendors calling out for your attention and letting you know what they have to offer, each trying their hardest to get you to buy from them. Just as you're not required to purchase what all the vendors are selling, you're not defined by your thoughts or required to listen to them. They're just passing through, sometimes containing things that you'll want and will be helpful to you and your life, sometimes not. You're the one listening to the calls, deciding which ones to engage with and which ones to let pass by. You're the one going through the market and deciding what you went there to buy and which items you're willing to leave behind. By recognizing this distinction, we unlock the power to observe our thoughts with clarity and detachment, empowering us to navigate the complexities of our inner world and to begin the process of coming home to ourselves.

The Process of Listening In

Listening in means tuning in to your thoughts without judgment. By being aware of our thoughts, we can recognize fear-based reactions and make conscious decisions aligned with our values. This practice helps us break free from automatic responses, leading to choices that are in our best interest. The following steps will guide you there.

Step 1: Set Aside Daily Time for Reflection

Find a quiet, comfortable space where you can be alone with your thoughts, free from distractions. Begin by taking a few deep breaths to center yourself and create a sense of calm. Spend at least 10 to 15 minutes each day in this space, allowing yourself to check in with your feelings and thoughts without judgment.

Step 2: Label Your Thoughts

As you delve into your inner world, practice labeling your thoughts based on their patterns. Identify thoughts that replay past events, catastrophize future scenarios, or criticize your actions. Take note of these thought patterns and messages without attaching judgment, recognizing them as common aspects of the human experience.

Step 3. Personify Your Inner Gremlin

Visualize your inner critic as a separate character within your mind, distinct from your true self. Give this inner gremlin a persona—an archetype that embodies its traits and tendencies. By externalizing this voice, you separate its criticisms from your authentic self and reclaim control over your self-image.

Step 4: Explore Core Beliefs

Listen closely to the messages conveyed by your inner gremlin, as they often reveal underlying beliefs about yourself. Reflect on whether these beliefs stem from fears, desires for approval, or feelings of inadequacy. Through this introspection, uncover the core beliefs that influence your self-perception and behavior.

Step 5: Discern Worthwhile Thoughts

Amid the mental chatter, practice discerning which thoughts best serve you and align with your values. Challenge yourself to sift through the noise, identifying thoughts that resonate with your aspirations. By consciously choosing which thoughts to engage with, you regain agency over your mental landscape, fostering clarity and purpose.

Step 6: Make Conscious Choices

Embrace everyday challenges as opportunities for growth and self-awareness. Before reacting impulsively, pause and reflect on your values and intentions. Ask yourself how you can respond with mindfulness and intention rather than defaulting to habitual reactions. By making conscious choices in each moment, you cultivate self-mastery and authenticity, leading to a more fulfilling and meaningful life journey.

Calm Kit Tool #4: Gremlin Discovery Technique

The Gremlin Discovery Technique is a psychological exercise aimed at identifying and personifying one's inner critic, often referred to as the gremlin. Here's how to practice the technique.

1. **Set the stage.** Find a quiet and comfortable space where you can engage in introspection without interruptions. You may want to have pen and paper handy to jot down notes or insights.

2. **Reflect on inner criticism.** Begin by reflecting on times when you've experienced self-doubt, self-criticism, or negative self-talk. Think about the thoughts and beliefs that arise in these moments and how they make you feel.

3. **Identify gremlin characteristics.** As you reflect on your inner critic, consider what characteristics or traits it possesses. Is it harsh, judgmental, perfectionistic, or fearful? Take note of any recurring themes or patterns in your self-criticism.

4. **Personify the gremlin.** Once you have a sense of your inner critic's characteristics, imagine giving it a physical form or persona. You might envision it as a small creature, a cartoon character, or even a familiar figure from literature or mythology. Get creative and trust your intuition.

5. **Engage in dialogue.** Once you've personified your gremlin, engage in a dialogue with it. You can do this through writing, visualization, or verbal communication. Ask your gremlin questions, such as:
   - What are you trying to protect me from?
   - Why do you say these things to me?
   - What do you need from me?

6. **Listen and reflect.** As you converse with your gremlin, pay attention to its responses and the emotions it evokes. Notice any insights or revelations that arise from this dialogue. Remember to approach the conversation with curiosity and compassion rather than judgment.

7. **Establish boundaries.** While it's important to acknowledge and understand your inner critic, it's also essential to establish healthy boundaries with it. Remind yourself that the gremlin's perspectives do not necessarily reflect reality or your true worth. Practice self-compassion and challenge negative self-talk when it arises.

8. **Integration and healing.** As you become more familiar with your gremlin and its motivations, work on integrating this awareness into your self-care practices. Cultivate self-compassion, challenge limiting beliefs, and seek support from trusted friends, family members, or mental health professionals if needed.

The Gremlin Discovery Technique can be a valuable tool for increasing self-awareness, challenging negative self-talk, and fostering self-compassion. By personifying your inner critic, you can develop a more compassionate and empowered relationship with yourself.

6 Cultivating Self-Love

A Gentle Reminder

You don't have to change a single thing to be worthy of the things you desire. Who you are right now, in this moment, is enough. I hope that one day you will begin to see that perfection is not a requirement of a well-lived life and that striving for perfection and holding yourself back until you get there is only keeping you from the life you deserve. Stop for a moment and recognize that without a single shift in who you are, you are enough, you are worthy, and you are deserving of whatever it is that your heart desires. Stop holding yourself back by holding yourself to impossible standards and start seeing the beauty that is you.

What Is Self-Love?

We're told that for us to be able to express love to others, we need first to learn to love ourselves. That sentiment ignores the fact that many of us grew up in households where self-love wasn't modeled but shame certainly was. We grew up in families where love was something to be earned and perfection was required to be deserving of that love. We were raised in a society that continually placed value and feelings of worth on external achievements and perceptions of others. For these reasons, it's understandable that the concept of self-love may seem foreign to many of us.

So, what is self-love? It's the understanding that there is beauty in all of us. There is a beauty that exists in the broken and the bruised parts, the parts that are quick to anger, the parts that feel things so deeply, and the parts that can't quite seem to get it right. In spite of and because of all of those parts of us, there is goodness that is worthy of love within each of us. And that goodness is not contingent on fixing or bettering any of those parts. Self-love is being able to look within without judgment and recognize that the perfectly imperfect being you are deserves love and kindness. The key to self-love is understanding that no amount of effort will ever make you any more worthy of love than you are right now. No deeds or actions will create a more worthy version of you, because worthiness is not dependent on anything but your mere existence. We exist in a world that constantly tells us that our worth is dependent on what we produce and that if we work hard and prove ourselves, then we'll be worthy. But this focus on external achievement as validation of worth creates a system in which we are constantly striving to be more rather than recognizing that we are enough.

Viewing your worth as inherent doesn't make you unwilling to grow and change and be of service to the world. It just allows you to do it in a way that is not in pursuit of something. It removes the striving and allows you to find gratitude and appreciation for the simplicity of being. This attitude creates a world that isn't driven by a selfish pursuit of achieving worthiness that requires others to be less worthy so you can feel like you are enough. No longer do you need to believe yourself better than someone else in order to feel your worth.

This viewpoint most likely contrasts with what you've been taught, so it makes sense to feel at odds with it. But removing that search for worthiness will allow you to be more productive, more impactful, more connected, and more authentic in your life.

Finding Space for Love

"Don't worry, I'm completely sober. I just sound drunk and tend to fall over a lot." Andrea's sharp wit and humor were on display from our first coaching session. Her ability to find levity in the face of difficult situations was refreshing and also clearly a tool formed over years of needing to explain herself to people who stared at her as she stumbled over her words and feet trying to get through the day. Her ability to light up a room and make your sides hurt from laughing was a superpower sculpted from some dark moments. If you didn't get the chance to sit and dig deeper, you would never know that beneath that smile was the chronic pain of a crippling disability that had accompanied her since she was a child as well as the heartbreak that came from the recent loss of her husband of 35 years.

During our years together, we explored many life topics and reached many goals, but one subject I was honored to get to hold space for was her experience of developing a sense of self-love. The word "no" was often the catalyst for Andrea to push through and prove to everyone that, despite her disability, she could conquer anything. She became a college graduate, a published author, a mother, a wife, and even joined a local softball team because her father offhandedly mentioned that running the bases would be too hard for her. To the world, she was an incredible success story: a woman who persevered through the pain of her disability and seemed to do more in one day than most people could in a week. While she couldn't hide the physical manifestations of her condition, she made it her mission not to let anyone know how it affected her. She created a life centered around accomplishing whatever she could and proving herself to be unstoppable, hoping it would gain her the love that was missing from within.

In this quest to be unstoppable, she wore herself down. No one saw that after each softball game came days of excruciating pain when she was unable to get out of bed. They didn't see her throwing up between classes at college, and they never saw her struggle to gain the strength to keep up with her two-year-old after falling for the tenth time that day. Andrea's pain was constant, and she always needed to adjust and move around it. The relationships, the jobs, the dreams she once had were all affected as she dealt with the pain. It took strength to put one foot forward, and beneath that strength was a hatred of herself for her perceived imperfections. Somewhere along the line, she had learned that for her to be accepted, respected, and loved, she needed to hide that pain and prove that she was extraordinary. She couldn't feel a sense of self-love, so she sought it from the world around her.

Andrea's sessions always seemed to move a mile a minute. She would launch into her week, her challenges, and her triumphs, and probe me for answers on how to tackle whatever she was focused on at the moment. As someone who works to help others find calm within their lives, this heightened energy and enthusiasm for life was fun to witness but often made me feel that she was running the sessions to avoid the reasons she hired me in the first place. I spent a lot of time in sessions just giving Andrea space and observing behaviors and energy, then gently probing to see how the tenets of mindfulness, the practice of meditation, or coaching philosophies might benefit her. It took several months working with Andrea before I could move beyond an action-oriented coaching model into the mindfulness-based model that I find brings the most clarity and connection.

Andrea logged on late for an online session one day, which was very unlike her, and I could immediately tell that there was a shift in her energy. Her demeanor was more subdued, and longer periods of silence replaced her usual weekly updates and probing questions. I always try to meet my clients where they are and show up for them in the way that best serves that moment. That day I could tell that Andrea needed a moment to breathe.

I asked if she would be open to moving through a simple mindfulness-based exercise to help center and ground her in the moment. With her consent, I led her through the process of sitting with the discomfort I could sense was present, beginning with a simple Body Scan (Chapter 2) and then an exploration of feelings.

As we got deeper into the meditation, I started to recognize the discomfort that was present and offered her the opportunity to begin to name it. Tears began to fall—something I had not seen from this woman who constantly exuded strength. I could also sense an urge to pull away. With her permission, I asked if she would be willing to sit with the discomfort of that moment and just allow herself to connect with the emotional experience and the thoughts that accompanied the feelings that were present. I invited her to give herself permission to not censor or avoid anything that was coming up for her. After a few moments, I had Andrea slowly move away from the thoughts, letting them fall as she tuned in deeper to the emotional experience and allowed herself to feel into the moment.

After she opened her eyes and returned to the space, we spent the rest of the session discussing what had come up during that exercise. She discovered that she couldn't remember the last time she let herself feel the discomfort, both physical and emotional, that she felt daily. She had taught herself that, to gain the love she needed, she had to disregard her constant pain in the presence of others and show only her tenacity and strength. Her impulse to hide pain and move through it had served her in the past, but ultimately it was keeping her from moving toward the life of freedom she envisioned for herself. Giving a voice to her pain, she recognized her feeling of unworthiness, of self-hatred, and of disappointment, and she had a deep desire to feel the love she had once felt from her late husband, Tom. Even as she constantly rushed to prove her worth, Tom let her know that his love was not conditional on any achievement and that she was more than enough. What she realized during our session was that with Tom's death, she'd lost the connection to the person who reminded her of her inherent worth, and she was killing herself trying to find it from anywhere but within.

As we ended the session, she asked if we could focus the next few sessions on cultivating a sense of self-love. She had no idea where to begin but recognized that it was the one thing that was going to save her from herself and bring her the peace that she was seeking.

A Reference Point for Love

During my own journey home to myself, I had a realization similar to Andrea's when I started to begin to listen in. I realized that I was perfectly capable of giving love, but finding it within just didn't seem possible. I wanted to begin to speak more gently to myself and see myself as someone of value and worth, but my ingrained patterns of thought were tough to shake, and any affirmations or kind words directed at myself felt phony. I often practiced Loving-Kindness, a meditation in which you extend well wishes of love, kindness, care, and compassion to different people or groups within your life through a series of phrases (Chapter 14). I was able to share these words with others easily, even those I'd had conflict with, but whenever it came back to me, I would feel disingenuous. That voice in my head would start identifying all the ways I was not worthy of hearing those words.

But one day during a meditation, my teacher took us through a visualization where we recognized a dear one and had them speak words of loving-kindness to us. Immediately I thought of my grandmother, who was one of the people I'd always felt deep and unconditional love from. She was the type of person to acknowledge your uniqueness, sing your praises to everyone she ever met, and let every one of grandchildren know how loved we were no matter what. On my last visit with her before she passed, she grabbed the hospice nurse and made sure to tell her how special I was. Even through her pain, she wanted to make sure that everyone in her life felt her love. I was unable to see my inherent good-ness, but she was fully aware of it and tried in every interac-tion to make sure I knew it. Picturing her and hearing her speak these words to me felt powerful, and for a brief moment during my meditation, they were able to drown out the critic in my head and let me feel a sense of love for myself.

I started playing with the concept of positive self-talk through the lens of my grandmother. Whenever I became aware that negative thoughts were rising, I paused for a moment and asked myself: Is this getting me closer to a place of self-acceptance or farther away? If a thought wasn't help-ful and was moving me away from the self-love I was trying to cultivate, I replaced it with an affirmation that came from her. Over time, her voice began to replace the gremlin voice (Chapter 5). Eventually, in those moments of need, I was able to feel that love coming from myself.

Visualizing Love

During our next session, I asked Andrea if she would be will-ing to work through a guided visualization with me that would include images of Tom and his love for her. She took a deep breath, knowing that things were about to get heavy, and agreed to give it a try.

We began with the 5-4-3-2-1 Calming Technique for Anxiety (Chapter 1). With her eyes open, she began to take in the room around her. Drawing awareness to her senses allowed her to come back to the present moment and ease the anxiety that was with her that morning. When every-thing began to settle, I asked her to find the nearest door to her and to keep the image of that door in mind as we went into the visualization.

With her eyes closed, she started to connect to her breath, and then I led Andrea through the next visualization.

Begin to recall the image of the door and then imagine that through that door walks Tom. Begin to see his face, notice the outline of his body and his hands. Start to feel his presence as he comes closer to you, and imagine that he sits down in front of you and reaches out to hold your hands. As you feel the weight of his hands, you look into his eyes and feel the deep connection of love that has always been there. And as you share this special moment, he begins to speak to you and says, *"You are good. There is nothing wrong with you, nothing that needs to be fixed. You are loved and you're going to be OK."*

Allow those words to land on you. Feel into the deep trust that you have for Tom and know that these words coming from him are true. Start to feel how they are held in your body, and take note of how it feels to be connected to them.

Now take your hand and place it on your heart and connect to that same feeling of love extended to you by Tom. Allow yourself to say these words directed to you: *"I am good. There is nothing wrong with me, nothing that needs to be fixed. I am loved and I'm going to be OK."*

Sit for a moment feeling what those words directed inward change within you. Let them land on you and know that these words coming from yourself are true.

I ended the visualization by inviting Andrea to thank Tom for loving her so deeply and for showing her how to love herself in his absence. After good-byes, I guided her back from the visualization and had her draw her awareness to her surroundings within the room before opening her eyes. As I welcomed her back, she opened her tearful eyes and told me that this was the closest she'd felt to home in a long time.

Connecting to Self-Love

The Self-Love Guided Visualization tends to elicit a deep emotional response. It serves to connect with someone in your life whom you trust and whom you recognize has a view of you that may be clearer than your own. Imagine your loved one sharing simple yet poignant words with you. At the same time, focus on the physical, emotional, and mental responses that come as you hear those words. These responses serve as reference points for what love and care can feel like. When turned inward, the responses can be guides for you to start to express self-love, kindness, and care to yourself.

As with all things, there is a process and practice to finding a sense of self-love. I've found that utilizing this Self-Love Guided Visualization daily allows people to connect with the feelings of love and to replace the gremlin voice within. Over time, when that voice begins to speak badly of you, ask what your dear one would say to you. Just allowing that counterpoint is enough to give you the awareness of thought and the ability to choose how to respond to it. By returning to the voice of a dear one and having their voice lead you, you slowly start to develop that voice as your own. People adopt the gremlin voice out of fear and external reinforcement of negativity; we can adopt the voice of self-love out of care and consideration for our own well-being.

Follow this five-step process to cultivate self-love.

Step 1: Identify Someone in Your Life You Deeply Care About

Take a moment to think of someone in your life whom you deeply care about. This could be a friend, family member, mentor, or anyone who has shown you unconditional love and support. If no one comes to mind immediately, consider imagining a younger version of yourself or even an animal that has brought you comfort and joy.

Step 2: Create a Daily Practice of Connecting with That Person

Make a commitment to connect with this person daily, even if it's just in your thoughts. Set aside a few minutes each day to think about them, express gratitude for their presence in your life, and reflect on the deep and meaningful connection you share. This daily practice will help you feel more connected and supported, even when the person is not physically present.

Step 3: Utilize Their Voice as a Guide Toward Self-Love

During your daily practice, use the Self-Love Guided Visualization, described next, to connect with the affirmations and kindness expressed by this person. Imagine them speaking words of love and encouragement directly to you, just as they would in real life. Notice how their words make you feel, and allow yourself to internalize their loving messages.

Step 4: Combat the Inner Critic with Their Loving Voice

Whenever your inner critic pops up, imagine what this special person would say if they heard you speaking that way about yourself. Visualize them offering words of kindness, reassurance, and belief in your worth. Replace the critical voice with their loving and supportive words, reminding yourself of the love and acceptance they have for you.

Step 5: Replace the Gremlin Voice with One of Love

Whenever you notice the gremlin voice creeping in, speaking unkindly or fostering self-doubt, consciously replace it with the voice of love and support from this special person in your life. Remind yourself that you are worthy of love and acceptance, just as they believe you to be. Cultivate a practice of self-compassion and gentleness, using their loving voice as a guide to greater self-love and acceptance.

Calm Kit Tool #5: Self-Love Guided Visualization

The Self-Love Guided Visualization technique is a mindfulness exercise designed to cultivate self-compassion and self-acceptance. It involves imagining a dear person in your life who embodies love and support and then directing their affirming words toward yourself. Here's how to do it.

1. **Identify someone you deeply care about.** Start by thinking of someone in your life whom you deeply care about and who has shown you unconditional love and support. This could be a friend, family member, mentor, or anyone who embodies kindness and compassion.

2. **Visualize their presence.** Close your eyes and imagine this person walking through a door and sitting in front of you. Picture their presence vividly in your mind's eye. Notice their facial expressions and body language and the warmth they radiate.

3. **Receive their affirmations.** Envision this person speaking directly to you, offering affirming and reassuring words. Hear them say phrases such as "You are good. There is nothing wrong with you, nothing that needs to be fixed. You are loved and you're going to be OK." Allow yourself to fully receive their words with an open heart.

4. **Notice your feelings and sensations.** As you hear these affirmations, pay attention to how they make you feel. Notice any emotions or sensations that arise within you. Allow yourself to experience these feelings without judgment, simply acknowledging them with compassion.

5. **Hold on to the positive feelings.** Hold on to the positive feelings of love, acceptance, and reassurance that arise during the visualization. Let them wash over you, enveloping you in a sense of comfort and security. Allow yourself to bask in the warmth of their love.

6. **Direct the affirmations toward yourself.** Now begin to direct these same affirmations toward yourself. Repeat them silently or out loud, addressing yourself with the same kindness and compassion that this special person has shown you. Say to yourself: "I am good. There is

nothing wrong with me, nothing that needs to be fixed. I am loved and I'm going to be OK."

7. **Embrace self-compassion.** Notice how it feels to offer yourself these words of affirmation and love. Allow yourself to fully receive them, acknowledging your inherent worthiness and deservingness of love and acceptance. Embrace a sense of self-compassion and self-acceptance.

By practicing this visualization regularly, you can cultivate a deeper sense of self-compassion, self-acceptance, and self-love. Drawing on the love and kindness of someone dear to you can serve as a powerful reminder of your own inherent goodness and worthiness of love.

7 Letting Go

Gentle Reminder

Whatever you're holding on to right now—whether it's a relationship, a job, a past experience, a grudge—if it's time to release the grip and start to create a life without it; let go. In letting go, you may experience fear, sadness, loneliness, or pain, even when you recognize that what you're holding on to no longer serves you. Know that those feelings aren't just from the anticipation of releasing that something or someone but also from releasing the future you had crafted for yourself in your mind. Go ahead and mourn the loss of that future. Let the sadness, fear, loneliness, and pain wash over you, and grieve for as long as you need. Once that grieving has begun, you give yourself the ability to slowly start to move forward toward a new future, one beyond your current situation that can be fully aligned with who you want to be in this world. It's there for you, but in order to get there, you need to let go.

Often the concept of letting go is connected to a feeling of giving up. We're afraid that by letting go, we relinquish our power and admit to the world that we've failed. But letting go is not waving the white flag of defeat; it's detaching ourselves from the need to control the outcome. It's recognizing that without controlling, possessing, or excessively identifying with something, we will be OK. Letting go is a practice of finding freedom and inner peace by releasing the bonds of attachment, which often lead to suffering and dissatisfaction.

Even when we know that letting go is the best option for us—when we carefully look at a situation from all sides and recognize that what we've been holding on to no longer serves us—stepping away can be difficult. The fear of losing what could have been feels like a death, so we hold on tightly to what is known, hoping that the envisioned future will come true, even when we know it won't. We would rather choose the comfort of the familiar than face the discomfort of letting go of that vision and stepping into a future we haven't yet imagined.

As humans, we're comfort-seeking machines, and often the quickest way to comfort is by returning to the perceived safety and security of the known. But avoiding discomfort doesn't necessarily provide a safer or more secure environment; it merely creates an environment of familiarity. It reinforces patterns that we are used to and keeps us surrounded by people and spaces that we know. But just because something is familiar doesn't mean that it is safe, healthy, or worth repeating.

If your avoidance of discomfort continually leads you back to old patterns of behavior or relationships that no longer serve you, it may be time to ask if that "comfort" is truly as valuable as you think it is. Look at the cost of that decision and determine if the perceived comfort found there is truly worth it. There is power in looking beyond the current situation and recognizing that the momentary discomfort of letting go will create far less discomfort than a lifetime of holding on and reliving situations that bring you harm and discontent.

Holding On

After the sudden end of her 15-year marriage, Stephanie reached out to me. The ending of the relationship wasn't her choice and was handled in an abrupt, clinical, and cold manner by her ex-husband, Mark. She felt completely blindsided. In an instant, her world went from being mapped out to a world where nothing was. She felt anger, fear, resentment, and at times a deep hatred for Mark. But even through all of that, she continued to try to hold on, longing to return to the familiarity of the life that they had built together.

Our first session together was roughly a year after her divorce was official. Stephanie had been seeing a therapist to process her initial grief and shock and had been referred to me to find ways to deepen her understanding of her emotions. Her goal for our time together was to learn to utilize mindfulness as a tool to navigate through the more difficult emotional experiences she had been facing and to begin to find herself again.

Telling Her Story

One of the first things that I do in sessions is allow clients to tell their stories. In life, there are few times when we have a fully captive and impartial person just listen to us, not judge or offer advice, but hold space as we let our story out into the world. Stephanie started by launching into her story, recalling with vivid detail the last moments in the house with her now ex-husband. After the papers were signed and the last boxes packed, she watched as he left her without a good-bye. As he drove away, she stood there holding their daughter and trying to figure out how she could care for them both in his absence. The situation was heavy and detailed, and I could sense that she was emotionally right back there as she retold the story.

I asked her to go back a little further and tell me what her marriage had been like. My aim was to get a glimpse into what she was leaving behind as she moved into this next phase of her life. She told me about a picture-perfect life. She had fallen in love with the boy from across the hall in her freshman year of college and had been with him through all of life's biggest moments. He was by her side during her father's death and had promised to always take care of her, no matter what. She detailed the wedding day until the day he walked out the door for the last time, and you could sense her deep love for him and the pain of losing him. There was a swirl of emotions, and she didn't know which one to grasp at any given moment. Sorting through the emotions and getting clear on a way forward was the goal, but getting there would take time and patience.

As the months went by, Stephanie took steps forward in her new life. She decorated her home as she had always wanted to and found comfort and excitement with each new piece of furniture that was just her style. She joined social groups and found a core group of friends to keep her company—friends separate from the friends she and Mark had shared. She challenged herself at work, and with the additional time when her daughter was away with her father, she networked. In fact, she was well on her way to a promotion. Stephanie was dedicated to moving forward and was doing everything she knew to create a new life for herself, but at night, at home, she would feel a longing to return to her old life. To the world she was the picture of a woman reclaiming her independence and thriving, but in the comfort of her weekly session she shared those nights of loneliness and let herself feel the anger and pain of it all.

My job as a coach was simply to hold space for Stephanie and help to open an awareness of her inner world and how it matched the world around her. During one session we started discussing the life she had built with Mark and how it matched with her values, needs, and desires. Through that lens, for the first time she was able to reveal dissatisfaction in the marriage. She spoke of her loneliness, her longing for more, and the sense that she was never enough. An outsider might think that she would have been relieved by her divorce. But still she was holding on, and her inability to let go was spinning her out of control. She wasn't holding on to the love; that had been gone for quite some time. She wasn't holding on to companionship; she had felt alone and isolated most days. She was holding on to the idealized version of what they had together and the future that she had created with him, the clarity of vision they had together for what their life would be one day. For 15 years they worked to build a future. Even when the life they had built was clearly not going to lead to that future, letting go felt like a loss too great to bear.

Crafting a New Vision

Stephanie had let go of so many parts of the relationship already and was moving on beautifully in many areas, but to truly move forward, she needed to mourn the loss of the future that the couple had planned for. She needed to craft a vision of a future without her ex-husband. Getting to that vision took time and effort, but along the way she found a way to come home to herself again and build a life from there.

The first thing that we worked through was mourning the loss of what could have been. I find that writing is a cathartic way to process emotions creatively. I gave Stephanie the homework assignment of revisiting the vision she had crafted with Mark and writing about what that future looked like, not sparing any details. The assignment included using the framework of breaking this vision into seven sections of life: family, career, health and wellness, social life, spiritual connection, emotional well-being, and love. The goal was to create a full picture of the life that she had been building, looking 15 years into the future and seeing where she had envisioned herself and her family at that point.

This assignment is never easy, and Stephanie came to our next session with tears already in her eyes. She told me that she had avoided the assignment until the night before when she finally got the courage to sit down and work through each section. I asked if she would be willing to read it to me, and she outlined in great detail every possible vision that she had for her future with Mark. She told me of her clear hopes and visions for what their life would be like together. From the time they were 18, they had planned on growing old together, watching their daughter grow up, and walking her down the aisle. They had planned to travel extensively. They even had picked out the house they would retire to. It made perfect sense that she was still attached to the vision. The comfort and stability that it created for her was worth holding on to, as the alternative was moving forward into the unknown.

As Stephanie allowed herself, for the first time, to let everything she was holding on to come to the surface, her process of letting go had begun. With it came a flood of tears, and she allowed herself to mourn the loss of that future. With any loss, the mourning process takes time, but it is important to recognize that one can mourn and move forward at the same time. While grieving the loss of their future plans may have stopped her in her tracks momentarily, the work of letting go continued.

One thing that I found interesting about my initial session with Stephanie was that her story began with Mark. The end of their relationship began her story, and when I asked her to go back in time, she told her story from the beginning of her relationship with Mark. She never mentioned her life before Mark. I never want to dive into childhood experiences, especially when trauma is involved. Trauma is best served in a therapeutic setting with a licensed therapist, but at times we can use younger versions of ourselves to better understand our current versions.

In our next session, I asked Stephanie if she would be willing to describe who she was growing up. I didn't need to hear specific details of her life; I was more interested in what she dreamed of, how she interacted with people, and what she loved. She thought back and told me of a quirky, vibrant, firecracker of a girl whose eyes lit up at the sight of city skylines and who could talk to a stranger about anything. She was silly and perhaps a bit naive but had big dreams and a huge heart.

As she thought back to this younger version of herself, in a way she began to embody her. I saw a lightness to Stephanie that I hadn't seen over the last few months. I asked if she would be willing to take on a new homework assignment this week, and, begrudgingly, she agreed, knowing that it would probably leave her a teary mess again. I tasked her with taking that same assignment, to identify the hopes and visions in the specified categories of life, but this time to do it from the point of view of that younger version of herself. To go back in time and begin to remember what she dreamed of and wanted more than anything but not filter it through her adult lens. I wanted this vision to be as playful as possible.

The following week's session started with that same lighthearted energy I'd seen when Stephanie described herself as a child. She could hardly contain her excitement. Not only had she finished the homework assignment, but she had picked up a giant posterboard and the fanciest and most glittery pins and Post-its to create a whimsical vision board. She filled in all the categories with photos she cut out from magazines and decorated it with hearts and stickers. The entire vision board was an embodiment of exactly the person she described in our last session.

We went through each section of the board, and while there were many hilariously outdated dreams, like marrying David Hasselhoff and driving around with him in a Ford Mustang, there were some beautiful dreams that had come true. She got to see herself become the kind of mom she always had wanted to be. She traveled the world, graduated college, and got to experience what true love felt like. And there were also some dreams that she had forgotten about that sparked something in her. She saw a chance to return to the free-spirited, lighthearted girl who always dreamed of living life large.

As we debriefed that day, I asked her to look at the two versions of her homework and to choose what she wanted to carry forward with her into her new vision and what she was willing to let go of. We sat and went through her childhood vision board one item at a time and left behind those that were no longer an option (sorry, David Hasselhoff). We crossed off anything that didn't align with who she was now, and she pointed to two items that she wanted to bring back into her life: a career and living in a big city.

Before her daughter was born, Stephanie had dreamed of working in fashion. Although she had used the artistic talents that she honed in college to create outfits for her daughter, she had put the dream of pursuing a career as a designer away long ago. While she was satisfied with the work that she was currently doing and clearly was excelling at it, looking back at those childhood ambitions stirred a desire to pursue her dream. She started to let herself imagine a life where her passion was at the forefront of her career. She also started to let herself return to that younger version who dreamed of living in the city. That had never been practical with Mark, but as she started to dream of a future that lit her up, she knew she desperately wanted to be in the bustle of a huge city.

We then looked at the list of the vision for her life with Mark and started with what she still wanted to keep. Those visions of watching her daughter grow and helping her become the most amazing version of herself would stay with her, even though it would look like coparenting rather than as a unit. The career ambitions would shift, and that house where she and Mark had planned on retiring would be replaced with a high-rise on the Upper West Side of New York.

As the vision she was crafting started to get clearer, Stephanie started to give herself permission to let go of the plans of growing old with Mark and stop holding on to hope that their love would rekindle. It was the first time she had let herself start to dream of a life without him, and in that moment there existed sadness for the loss of what could have been paired with an excitement of what was possible.

Stephanie began to craft a vision that was true to who she was now, holding on to the parts of her life that were meaningful and important and adding new hopes and dreams alongside them. This new vision gave her guidance and direction as she moved forward. Whereas before she was just throwing herself at the idea of change, she was now carefully creating a life that she wanted to be living.

When we came together for our next session, Stephanie was excited to share that she had started to take steps toward her new vision. She was careful not to make rash decisions and throw herself into something for the sake of change, as she had done before. She walked me through a list of actionable items that would help to lead her toward where she ultimately wanted to be. Her first step was to take a trip to Manhattan and let herself be inspired by the city. She wanted to take in the fashion and see how it might feel to wake up there each day. It was a small step, but one that let her begin to explore this new vision while starting to let go of the old.

The Process of Letting Go

Navigating significant life changes, such as divorce, the loss of a job, or the unexpected death of a loved one, requires acknowledging the loss of a once-cherished future while embracing the opportunity to redefine your path. The Future-Mapping Technique outlined in this chapter guides you through a comprehensive process of mourning, reflection, and forward thinking, incorporating key aspects of a well-rounded life.

Step 1: Articulating the Current Vision

Reflect on the envisioned future associated with what you are letting go of, considering each of the seven key areas of life:

- **Family.** Describe the envisioned family structure, dynamics, and shared aspirations.
- **Career.** Detail career goals, aspirations, and envisioned professional accomplishments.
- **Health and wellness.** Reflect on health goals, lifestyle choices, and overall well-being.
- **Social life.** Consider social connections, friendships, and community involvement.
- **Spiritual connection.** Explore beliefs, practices, and the role of spirituality in your envisioned future.
- **Emotional well-being.** Acknowledge emotional needs, coping mechanisms, and mental health considerations.
- **Love.** Describe the dynamics, aspirations, and shared experiences within romantic relationships.

Step 2: Reconnecting with Your Younger Self

Visualize your younger self, free from current constraints, and recall past aspirations in each key area of life. Reflect on the dreams and goals you held for the seven key areas of life.

Step 3: Integrating Past and Present Visions

First, compare your current and past visions, identifying elements to retain and those to release in each key area of life. Then determine which aspects of the past resonate with your present values and aspirations, considering the seven key areas of life.

Step 4: Crafting a New Future Vision

Envision a future that transcends the past, incorporating elements from both past and present visions in each key area of life. Describe your holistic future vision, encompassing the seven key areas of life.

Step 5: Detailing the Future Vision

First, set specific goals and intentions for each key area of life within your new future vision, ensuring balance and alignment with your values and aspirations.

Then create a roadmap for achieving your envisioned future, incorporating actionable steps for growth and fulfillment in the seven key areas of life.

This Future-Mapping Technique empowers people to honor their past while embracing the potential of a new future. By integrating past wisdom and present aspirations, we can chart a course toward holistic well-being, resilience, and fulfillment.

Calm Kit Tool #6: Calm Space Visualization

Visioning isn't just about setting goals and achieving dreams; it can also be a powerful tool for finding calm and inner peace. By visualizing a peaceful and tranquil future, you can create a mental sanctuary you can retreat to whenever you need to find calm amid the chaos of everyday life. Here's how to do it:

1. **Set the scene.** Find a quiet and comfortable space where you can relax without distractions. Close your eyes and take a few deep breaths to center yourself and clear your mind.

2. **Imagine your ideal sanctuary.** Visualize a place where you feel completely calm and at peace. It could be a secluded beach, a peaceful forest, a serene mountaintop, or any other tranquil setting that resonates with you. Use all your senses to bring this place to life in your mind's eye.

3. **Engage your senses.** As you visualize your ideal sanctuary, engage all your senses to make the experience as vivid and immersive as possible. Imagine the sound of gentle waves lapping against the shore, the scent of fresh pine trees, the feel of soft sand beneath your feet, and the taste of crisp, clean air.

4. **Feel the calm wash over you.** Allow yourself to fully immerse in the sense of calm and tranquility that surrounds you in your mental sanctuary. Feel the tension melting away from your body as you soak in the peaceful atmosphere. Let go of any worries or stressors, even if just for a moment.

5. **Set your intentions.** While in this state of calm, take a moment to set your intentions for finding peace and tranquility in your everyday life. Affirm to yourself that you deserve to experience calm and that you have the power to cultivate it within yourself.

6. **Anchor the feeling.** Before you end your visualization, take a moment to anchor the feeling of calm within yourself. Repeat a simple mantra or affirmation, such as "I am calm, I am centered, I am at peace," to reinforce the sense of tranquility within you.

7. **Return to your sanctuary.** Whenever you need to find calm in your life, return to your mental sanctuary through visualization. Close your eyes, take a few deep breaths, and transport yourself back to that peaceful place. Allow yourself to reconnect with the sense of calm and inner peace that you've cultivated.

By using visioning as a tool to find calm, you can create a sanctuary within your mind that you can access whenever you need to escape the stresses of everyday life. It's a simple yet powerful practice that can help you cultivate a sense of inner peace and tranquility, no matter what challenges you may be facing.

8 Heading Home

A Gentle Reminder

In order to come home to yourself, you have to stop avoiding those parts of yourself that you feel aren't good enough. So often you're hiding not just from the world but also from yourself. You hope that if you push those parts of you down deep enough or keep them in the dark for long enough, they'll magically go away. The truth is that no matter how much you hide from them, those parts of you are still there, whether you shine a light on them or not, and they tend to grow even in the darkness.

Coming home to yourself starts with allowing yourself to be present to every part of you. This is the hard bit that you—and most people—want to bypass. You want to instantly jump to that sense of self-acceptance and love, but the years you've spent

(continued)

97

hiding parts of yourself from the world means that you don't even understand what it truly feels like to live as yourself.

Leaping from avoidance of self to acceptance of self would be like marrying someone you haven't had the chance to get to know. Initially that marriage wouldn't flow with love and acceptance. You would need time to allow that person into your life, get to know them, let them be present, and start to walk through life with you. Then you could start to develop that sense of love and acceptance that would lead to a healthy marriage, but you need to allow them to be in your life first.

As you continue on this journey home, start to build that relationship with all the different parts of yourself. Not just the parts that feel acceptable, but those that feel shameful and dark, that you have locked away, and that you can't yet accept. Let them be there, get to know them, and let them know that they are a part of you and you're learning to love them.

One of the first questions we ask when meeting someone for the first time is "Where's home?" To most people, it's the simplest of questions and a chance to share a bit of history without getting in too deep. Learning where someone grew up can give you a picture of their life—their cultural background and upbringing—and often can serve as a point of connection between you and that person. It serves as a common ground that you can both relate to or discuss aspects of, fostering a sense of familiarity, understanding, and rapport.

I always hated that question, however. I didn't have a simple answer that would provide that point of connection to others. I was forced to choose one of the places I had lived or let them in on the more personal elements of my early life and share a long, depressing story. I'd lived many places, but not many felt like home. When I was in college, I remember hearing friends talk about how excited they were to go home for the holidays and how connected they were to the things that made them feel at home. They weren't referring just to the physical home they grew up in but to the sense of belonging, comfort, and emotional attachment that came from where they grew up. Others had a personal connection within the places they called home, and I hadn't felt that for quite some time. Even when I did go to visit, I still longed for a place to call home.

Finding Home Within

Just as I was longing for a sense of belonging and to experience the emotional connection of home, I was missing home within myself as well. I had been practicing mindfulness for several years and meditated every day, journaled, educated, and took care of myself more than I ever had. But while I was noting the positive changes in my life—and other people were as well—I kept waiting for a moment of enlightenment or a feeling that everything was right. I would have days when I felt aligned and connected and others where my anxiety spiked and I'd feel right back where I started. Would I ever find that feeling of home that I was looking for?

Then one day I stumbled on an old talk by Thích Nhất Hạnh, the famous Vietnamese monk, on YouTube, and in it he was talking about being content with impermanence. Our goal should be to find a place where we are able to fully accept the fact that nothing will last. He explained that holding on and trying to make permanent that which is impermanent will only lead to suffering. There is a beauty in impermanence when you recognize that without impermanence, children could never grow into smart and capable young adults and oppressive regimes could not change. When you accept impermanence, you begin to recognize the beauty that exists in the moments of change that occur throughout life and allow those moments of change to take place rather than fighting against them.

I realized that I was trying to make those days when I truly felt at home with myself last forever. I wasn't allowing the beauty of change to exist, and I was holding on tightly to what I perceived as good. When I allowed myself to let go, I started to recognize that even when change occurred and I started to feel lost and scared, that feeling wasn't permanent. In letting go of the attachment to permanence, I could always find my way back home to myself.

Heading Home

I learned that coming home to yourself doesn't occur all at once but through a series of moments. I started noting those moments in my journal to remind myself of what it felt like to recognize a part of home that I wanted to remember. Although there were many different moments when I felt a sense of coming home to myself, they all centered around

five key aspects. Please note that the moments may dif-
fer for you.

Here are the moments and what I found:

- **Self-awareness.** You stop for a moment and realize that things feel quieter and the voices that once kept you at a distance and rushing into old patterns triggered by the world around you have paused. In that quiet you feel an awareness of your emotions, your thoughts, and your impulses but recognize that there's choice now. You're no longer living life reacting but are consciously choosing how you want to show up. You feel a sense of control and a sense of surrender.

- **Self-acceptance.** You pass by a mirror and find that instead of critiquing your reflection, you smile, seeing the perfectly imperfect version of you smiling back. You find yourself enjoying connection with friends and loved ones and no longer feel the need to hide yourself from the world and fix your flaws before you're ready to be with them. Your perceived weaknesses or vulnerabilities no longer control your mind.

- **Self-compassion.** You make a mistake and find that in place of the cruel voice that once admonished you for your stupidity, a gentle and loving voice helps you pick up the pieces and move forward. You notice that in the same way that those closest to you have shared loving-kindness with you, you now are sharing loving-kindness with yourself.

- **Authenticity.** You're asked for your opinion on something and find that instead of scanning the room to see how others want you to respond, you share your opinion freely. Those choices and next steps become easier as you recognize that you have a clear understanding of what you value and believe and are living a life that is aligned with those values.

* **Inner peace.** In the middle of a chaotic scene with the world spinning around you, you find that you're able to settle into a sense of stillness as you watch it spin. A calm contentment resides within you, and you no longer have a desire to be anywhere but where you are nor anyone but who you are.

The change doesn't happen all at once, but slowly these moments meet you through the conscious effort to return to a space of comfort, safety, and belonging. Coming home to yourself is a journey of self-discovery, growth, and transformation, and it involves creating a nurturing and supportive relationship with yourself. It's about reconnecting with the deepest parts of who you are and finding solace, strength, and wholeness within yourself.

Stay open to the moments of change, continue to invest in yourself, find a space of calm, and make a daily habit of connecting back to yourself. It may take time, but go slowly and be patient with yourself. One day you'll recognize that you're home.

The Process of Heading Home

Heading home is a five-step process.

Step 1: Develop Self-Awareness

Begin your journey by cultivating a deep understanding of your thoughts, feelings, and behaviors. Take time for introspection and reflection, recognizing patterns and triggers that influence your actions.

Step 2: Find Self-Acceptance

Embrace all aspects of yourself, including your strengths, weaknesses, imperfections, and vulnerabilities. Practice self-acceptance without judgment or criticism, acknowledging your inherent worthiness and deservingness of love.

Step 3: Cultivate Self-Compassion

Treat yourself with kindness, understanding, and empathy, especially during difficult times or when facing challenges. Practice self-compassion by extending the same care and support to yourself that you would offer to a dear friend.

Step 4: Embrace Authenticity

Live in alignment with your true values, beliefs, and aspirations. Be genuine and authentic in your thoughts, words, and actions, expressing yourself honestly and openly without fear of judgment.

Step 5: Nurture Inner Peace

Cultivate a sense of inner calm, contentment, and fulfillment. Let go of external pressures and expectations, focusing instead on finding peace within yourself and living in harmony with the present moment.

Calm Kit Tool #7: Self-Compassion Journal

One tool for developing self-compassion is the Self-Compassion Journal. This practice involves regularly writing about your experiences, thoughts, and emotions with a focus on cultivating self-kindness, understanding, and acceptance. Here's how you can use the Self-Compassion Journal as a tool for building self-compassion:

1. **Set aside time.** Dedicate a specific time each day or week to engage in your journaling practice. Find a quiet and comfortable space where you can reflect without distractions.

2. **Reflect on experiences.** Begin each journaling session by reflecting on your recent experiences, both positive and negative. Consider moments of difficulty, challenge, or self-criticism as well as instances of success, joy, and growth.

3. **Express emotions.** Allow yourself to express your emotions freely on the pages of your journal. Write about how you're feeling without judgment or censorship. Use descriptive language to capture the nuances of your emotional experience.

4. **Practice self-compassion.** As you write, consciously practice self-compassion by offering yourself kindness, understanding, and acceptance. Treat yourself as you would a close friend who is going through a similar experience. Use compassionate language and affirmations to support yourself.

5. **Challenge negative thoughts.** Notice any self-critical or negative thoughts that arise during your journaling practice. Challenge these thoughts by offering yourself alternative perspectives and reframing your inner dialogue with self-compassion.

6. **Celebrate progress.** Take time to celebrate your progress and accomplishments, no matter how small. Acknowledge moments of growth, resilience, and self-care. Celebrating

your successes can reinforce feelings of self-worth and empowerment.

7. **Practice gratitude.** End each journaling session by expressing gratitude for yourself and your journey. Write down things you appreciate about yourself, moments of kindness you've shown to others, or aspects of your life that bring you joy and fulfillment.

By consistently using your Self-Compassion Journal, you will gradually develop greater self-compassion, resilience, and emotional well-being. Over time, you may notice increased self-acceptance, reduced self-criticism, and a deeper sense of connection and empathy toward yourself and others.

9

Meditations and Daily Habits for Coming Home to Yourself

This chapter is crafted to assist you in nurturing a deeper connection with yourself and fostering self-love, self-empathy, self-kindness, and self-care through meditative practices and daily habits. These practices are not only about finding solace in moments of need but also about weaving mindfulness into the fabric of your daily existence.

Meditations for Coming Home to Yourself

The next three meditations serve as tools for you to begin the journey of coming home to yourself. The Mindful Awareness of Thought Meditation involves observing thoughts without judgment, allowing them to arise and pass without attachment. This awareness allows you to begin to accept and show compassion toward yourself. The Self-Love Meditation nurtures a positive relationship with yourself by directing loving-kindness inward, offering affirmations of worthiness and acceptance gained from a connection with a loved one. The Heart-Centered

Meditation guides you to connect with the innate wisdom and compassion of the heart. By tapping into the heart's wisdom, you can begin to cultivate a sense of inner peace, authenticity, and alignment with your true essence. Together, these practices offer tools that promote a sense of self-love.

Mindful Awareness of Thought Meditation

The Mindful Awareness of Thought Meditation guides participants to find stillness and return to the present moment by letting go of past worries and future fears. With closed eyes or a soft gaze, individuals focus on the breath, exploring four types of thought: rehearsing, rehashing, catastrophizing, and judging. They allow their minds to wander freely before labeling and categorizing thoughts without judgment. Through a brief Body Scan, participants redirect attention to physical sensations, fostering self-awareness and mindful redirection. Regular practice can lead to improved focus, reduced stress, and a greater ability to stay present amid mental busyness, promoting feelings of connection, calmness, and groundedness.

> Find a space of stillness and return to the present moment, letting the worries of yesterday slip away, the fears of tomorrow drop, and connect back to the here and now. Let your body settle, connect to your surroundings, and let yourself let go.
>
> If it feels right and safe to do so, go ahead and close your eyes or have a soft focus with your eyes gazing downward. Start to connect to the breath, breathing in and breathing out.
>
> Begin to cultivate an awareness of thought. Allow yourself to be still for a moment and let your mind

run. Over the next few moments, let it wander in whatever direction it wants to go, not censoring or filtering it in any way. Just pause and let the mind be free. [Spend 2 minutes thinking mindlessly.]

Now come back to center and start to become aware of those thoughts that were freely flowing. As the thoughts come in, become aware of what type of thought you might be experiencing: Are you rehearsing, rehashing, catastrophizing, or judging? Without judgment, allow yourself once again to experience that thought and then label each one. [Spend 2 minutes labeling thoughts.]

Start to draw the awareness back to the body. Begin to check in with each part of you, from the head down to the toes, and note if there are any areas of tension or tightness. As you do so, note when thoughts arise and distract you from the body. Label each of these thoughts and make the conscious choice to redirect your attention to your body, letting the thoughts pass by like clouds in the sky. Continue to scan through the body and remove any judgment or frustration that may be present as thought comes in. There's nothing inherently wrong with thought; you're just practicing the act of awareness and redirection. [Spend 2 minutes redirecting thoughts to the body.]

Begin to come back fully into the moment, connecting back to the breath as you breathe in and breathe out. Start to become aware of the space around you. Experience all of your senses. When it feels right to do so, flutter your eyes open, and enter back into the space you are in, connected and calm.

Self-Love Meditation

The Self-Love Meditation is a practice that helps cultivate a deep sense of love, acceptance, and compassion toward oneself. Research suggests that practicing self-love can improve self-esteem, reduce anxiety and depression, and enhance overall well-being. By connecting with the unconditional love within, we can heal past wounds, release self-judgment, and embrace ourselves with kindness and compassion. This guided visualization offers a safe and nurturing space to come home to ourselves, reconnecting with the inherent worth and value that resides within each of us.

Start by settling in and taking in the space around you, noting the shapes, the colors, the figures, and hearing the sounds. Be fully present in this moment. As you take in your surroundings, locate the door nearest to you. Remember that door, then come back to the center. If it feels right and safe to do so, close your eyes or keep a gentle focus with your eyes gazing downward.

From this space, begin to imagine a person you care deeply about, someone you love, the mere thought of whom or mention of their name lights you up. Now imagine that person walking in through the door you noted. They come into the room and sit down in front of you. They hold your hands and look into your eyes, and you instantly feel that love and connection radiating from their being. Look into their eyes and hear the words that they say:

You are good.
There is nothing wrong with you,

nothing that needs to be fixed.
You're going to be OK.

Hold on to that space of love and allow those words to wash over you. [Be with that love for 2 minutes.]
Now take your hand and place it on your own heart. Feel into its beating and feel into that sense of love that was just gifted to you by that dear one. Say to yourself:

I am good.
There's nothing wrong with me,
nothing that needs to be fixed.
I'm going to be OK.

Allow those words to land on you, just as the words from that person did, and feel into a sense of care and compassion and unconditional love for yourself. Be with that self-love for 2 minutes.]
Imagine that person standing up to leave. Give them a big hug good-bye. Hold on to everything that they have given you, knowing that you can always return to use them as the reference point of what it feels like to experience love. Know that you can always return that felt sense of love for yourself.
As the person exits and the door closes, feel that sense of love. Open your eyes, taking in the space around you again and recognizing that the feeling remains.
Take that feeling with you today as you enter back into the world connected and calm.

Heart-Centered Meditation

The Heart-Centered Meditation helps participants connect with the wisdom and guidance of our hearts. Research suggests that heart-centered practices can reduce stress, improve emotional well-being, and enhance intuition. By tuning in to the wisdom of our hearts, we can access a deeper understanding of ourselves and our true desires. This meditation offers a space to come home to ourselves, reconnecting with the love, wisdom, and guidance that resides within our hearts. As we cultivate a deeper connection to our hearts, we can navigate life's challenges with greater clarity, compassion, and resilience, fostering a sense of peace and harmony within ourselves and in our interactions with others.

Allow yourself to settle into a space of comfort and stillness. Allow yourself to sink down into what's beneath you. Feel into the weight of your body as it rests on the chair or cushion, and feel into the heaviness of the body as you allow yourself to root down. And as you feel into that rooting from below, begin to feel into a lightness in your upper body, almost as if your chest and shoulders can rise to the ceiling and float away. Between the rooting and the rising, begin to connect to the centermost space of your body: your heart.

Place your hands on top of your heart and for the next few moments connect with its beating. Feel into the blood pumping through your body, and begin to breathe in connection with those heartbeats. Breathe in and breathe out, softening with each breath and settling into a gentle connection with your heart. [Allow 2 minutes of heart-connected breathing.]

Now begin to shift your awareness to the heart center, and begin to imagine that your heart is a mechanism that can breathe on its own. With each inhale, see a growing of your heart within your chest. Come back to center with each exhale. Feel the growing expansion of your heart within your chest as you breathe in and allow it to settle back into the heart center with each exhale. [Allow 2 minutes of focused breathing, imagining your heart growing and shrinking.]

Now begin to envision a radiant light glowing from within your heart. With each inhale, watch that light get brighter and fill the entirety of your chest. Notice the dimming of that light at the bottom of each breath as you release the air fully. Imagine this light expanding and growing brighter, filling your chest with warmth and love. As you exhale, begin to imagine any tension or stress present within your body today simply melting away, allowing a deep sense of peace and relaxation wash over you in the warm glow of the heart. [Allow 2 minutes of breathing connected to the light of the heart.]

As that warm glow from your heart continues to be present, take a moment to silently ask the heart for guidance or wisdom. Connect with the question that you need to answer in this moment. Allow any

(continued)

thoughts begin to arise naturally, letting the heart speak its wisdom to you. Let yourself trust in that innate wisdom and intuition coming from within and give yourself permission to simply listen. [Allow 2 minutes of heart-centered listening.]

As the answers you need become clear, feel into a sense of love and compassion flowing inward. Give yourself a chance to experience kindness, care, compassion, and love for yourself. Holding on to that love and compassion with the wisdom that your heart has shared, begin to return to the space. When it feels right to do so, flutter your eyes open, taking in the space around you, and enter back connected and calm.

Daily Habits for Coming Home

Incorporate these habits into your daily routine to help you on your journey home to yourself. They are a combination of self-care and self-reflection and will help you continue to gain a deeper understanding of self and how you desire to show up in the world.

Daily Self-Reflection Practice

Daily Self-Reflection is a powerful habit that empowers you to engage in a dialogue with yourself, fostering self-awareness and nurturing a deeper connection with your inner wisdom. Dedicate a few moments each day to this transformative practice, carving out a quiet space where you can be with your thoughts undisturbed. Begin by grounding yourself with a series of deep breaths, inviting a sense of calm and centeredness in. As you reflect on the events, emotions, and experiences of the day, observe any recurring patterns, emotions, or areas of tension that surface. Pose open-ended inquiries to yourself, probing into your emotional, physical, and mental states. Express gratitude for the day's blessings, examine challenges faced, and extract valuable lessons from your encounters. Whether you are journaling or performing quiet contemplation, honor your reflections with gentleness and compassion, embracing yourself with kindness and understanding. Conclude your Daily Self-Reflection Practice by crafting an intention or affirmation that resonates with your values and aspirations, guiding you toward a path of self-fulfillment and growth.

Examples of open-ended questions to ask yourself and journal on are:

- How am I feeling emotionally, physically, and mentally?
- What am I grateful for today?
- What challenges did I face, and how did I respond to them?
- What can I learn from today's experiences?

Daily Intention-Setting Practice

Setting intentions aligned with your vision for life empowers you to clarify your values, channel your focus, and manifest your aspirations into reality. Kickstart each day by immersing yourself in this ritual, seeking out that calm space where you can find stillness for a few moments. Ground yourself with a series of deep breaths, allowing the rhythm of your breath to anchor you in the present moment. Delve into the depths of your long-term goals, values, and aspirations, discerning what truly resonates with your desires. From this place of clarity, craft an intention for the day that aligns with your overarching vision for your life. Express your intention in the present tense, making it feel positive and powerful and as if it's already unfolding before your eyes. Envision yourself embodying this intention with clarity and conviction, and lean into what it feels like to be experiencing this in life. Carry this intention close to your heart throughout the day, allowing its guiding light to illuminate your path and infuse your thoughts, actions, and decisions with purpose and meaning.

Examples of daily intentions are:

- Today I intend to approach challenges with grace and resilience, knowing that each obstacle is an opportunity for growth and learning.
- My intention for today is to cultivate gratitude and appreciation for the abundance that surrounds me, recognizing the beauty in both big and small moments.
- I set the intention to prioritize self-care and nourish my mind, body, and spirit with kindness, compassion, and nurturing practices throughout the day.

Daily Acts of Self-Care

Daily Acts of Self-Care are essential to nourish your mind, body, and soul and to create a sense of balance and harmony in your life. Make self-care a priority by scheduling time each day for activities that nourish and rejuvenate you. Create a self-care routine that includes activities such as meditation, reading, bathing, spending time in nature, or enjoying a hobby. Listen to your body and mind, and choose activities that replenish your energy and bring you joy and fulfillment. Practice mindfulness during your self-care activities, savoring each moment and fully immersing yourself in the experience. Set boundaries and prioritize self-care, even when life gets busy or stressful. Be gentle with yourself and let go of perfectionism, allowing self-care to be a nourishing and nurturing practice rather than a chore. Reflect on how each self-care activity makes you feel, and adjust your routine as needed to meet your evolving needs and preferences.

PART 3

Honoring Connection

10 Understanding Empathy

grasp of their struggles, challenges, and triumphs. This understanding of their perspective opens the door to empathy, fostering a deeper connection and a sense of shared humanity. By stepping into their shoes and seeing the world through their eyes, you gain insight into the complexities of their experiences and discover how to find common ground.

Many components are required to build and maintain solid relationships. Communication, trust, support, and love are all necessary and require time and attention. If forced to choose the one component I feel is most vital to deepening human connection, it is empathy. Empathy is necessary for relationships of all types to succeed. Whether it's an intimate relationship with a partner, a professional relationship with a coworker or boss, a relationship with family and friends, or even passing relationships with strangers we encounter briefly, empathy is the foundation to create understanding and connection.

In simplest terms, the word "empathy" refers to the act of putting oneself in someone else's shoes and being able to share their feelings. Empathy goes beyond mere sympathy, providing a passive acknowledgment of one's emotions and allowing for an active engagement with another's experience. Sympathy is a nod of recognition from a distance; empathy extends a hand and walks alongside the other through their joys and sorrows.

Empathy is rooted in presence and compassion. To be empathetic, we must actively engage with the present moment to seek to understand the emotional experience of another. Presence is necessary to learn their story and gain an understanding of how they operate within the world and why they make the decisions they do. In addition, compassion helps to provide an open and nonjudgmental space to inquire about their experiences so we can deeply understand their story. It's compassion that compels us to share in the journey and meet them where they are emotionally.

Relationships progress through different stages, and empathy is required to help us navigate through the intricacies of each stage.

During the initial stage of forming a relationship, empathy is crucial for building trust and understanding. By empathizing with one another, individuals can connect on a deeper level, listen attentively, and respond with care and compassion. Doing this sets the groundwork for a solid and meaningful connection.

In times of conflict or strain, empathy plays a vital role in repairing relationships. It allows individuals to understand each other's perspectives, acknowledge the choices that led to the disagreement, and move past blame or judgment. Through empathetic communication, couples can work toward reconciliation and strengthen their bonds.

As relationships evolve, empathy continues to be essential for growth and maintenance. By empathizing with each other's emotions and needs, partners can offer support, celebrate successes, and navigate challenges together. This ongoing practice of empathy fosters a strong and resilient connection, enriching the relationship over time.

The absence of empathy can have far-reaching consequences, leading to challenges like conflict, division, and societal injustices. Without the ability to understand and share the feelings of others, individuals may prioritize their own interests at the expense of others, perpetuating in equality and fostering a sense of isolation. To address these challenges, it is essential to strengthen our capacity for empathy. By learning to empathize with others, we can bridge divides and foster understanding. Empathy enables us to recognize the humanity in others, regardless of differences, and to work toward solutions that benefit all members of society. In today's divided world, the cultivation of empathy is more important than ever. It's through empathy that we can overcome divisions, build connections, and create a future where everyone's needs are valued and respected.

The Importance of Perspective

It's important to note that perspective is everything when it comes to cultivating empathy. Perspective requires you to put your own version of the story aside and see the world through someone else's eyes. Putting yourself in someone else's shoes doesn't mean seeing the situation in terms of how *you* would respond. It means allowing yourself to understand the situation from their perspective and gain an understanding of their feelings through the lens from which they see the world. The moment you begin to reference your own beliefs, judgments, and worldview, you've lost the ability to imagine what someone else would do in the situation. All you're doing is imagining what *you* would do. True empathy demands a willingness to listen, observe, and understand someone's situation without imposing our own worldview onto the situation. By embracing this approach, we can foster deeper connections and a greater sense of understanding with those around us.

Each of us carries a unique set of lived experiences that shape our perceptions and interactions with the world. These experiences act as filters through which we interpret events, form beliefs, and navigate our daily lives. Several factors contribute to the complexity of our worldview. These may include:

- **Upbringing.** The environment in which we are raised plays a significant role in shaping our worldview. Family dynamics, parental beliefs, and cultural traditions all contribute to the lens through which individuals see the world.
- **Culture.** Cultural influence, such as customs, traditions, and societal norms, play a profound role in shaping our perspective. Cultural values and beliefs inform attitudes toward topics like family, community, religion, and authority.
- **Education.** Formal education and life experiences serve as powerful influences on perspective. Academic teachings, exposure to diverse viewpoints, and personal growth experiences contribute to the formation of our worldview.
- **Personal experiences.** Individual experiences, both positive and negative, leave an indelible mark on perspective. Life events, relationships, and challenges shape our beliefs, values, and attitudes toward ourselves and others.

Learning the intricacies of someone's story takes time and energy. Doing so requires you to create a nonjudgmental environment of openness and compassion in which you can explore these experiences, ask or ponder thoughtful questions, and be willing to listen intently and objectively. And with all things, be patient and kind; many people do not find it easy to share their story.

Empathy in Action

Barbara contacted me to schedule a session after listening to an episode of my podcast in which I discussed the Portuguese word *saudade*. The term refers to an experience of feeling the love that remains after loss or separation from someone or something meaningful to you. It's not quite sadness but rather a feeling of deep emotional longing accompanied by the gratitude of having experienced it at all. It encompasses a triggering of the senses that makes the experience live again for a moment. Saudade perfectly described the feeling Barbara could not quite place. She hoped to work through ways to honor both sides of the feeling while trying to move forward in her life. It had been nine years since her husband had passed away. Now, as she entered her late seventies, she was finally settling into being on her own, but that feeling of longing.

We spent several months working together. Barbara made some beautiful changes and noted how settled she felt in the life she was living and the ease that was present. So, it came as a bit of a surprise to me when she came into session and informed me that she had agreed to go on a date that weekend. One of the women from church, whom she referred to as quite the busybody, had been pestering her for months to meet a friend of hers whom she swore was a perfect match for Barbara. On a day Barbara was feeling particularly cheerful, she agreed that she would be willing to meet for a casual coffee date. She was surprisingly calm and unfazed by the prospect of dating for the first time since she was twenty-two. She said that she didn't have her hopes up, but she was feeling confident about herself recently, and the worst that could happen would be a bad conversation and a decent cup of coffee.

She came back the next week and mentioned that the coffee was terrible but the conversation was great. Phil was kind and compassionate and was interested in learning about her and her life and was open to share about his. He had lost his wife two years earlier, and they connected over what that experience was like for each of them. But they also shared other parts of their stories. By the time the date had wrapped up, they had already agreed to go on a second date, dinner this time. I asked if she was feeling nervous or having any conflicting feelings, but besides the fact that having a crush in her late seventies feeling odd, something about it felt comfortable.

The relationship continued to grow. A few dates turned into several months of dating and a very meaningful connection for Barbara and Phil. Barbara never brought anything regarding the relationship into our coaching sessions. She would give me updates and was very happy but wanted to continue to focus on inner work and developing her mindfulness practice.

About six months into their relationship, Barbara came into the session, let out a loud sigh, and asked if we could focus on Phil. She was having a hard time understanding some of his behaviors. Although she was trying to be patient, she was also scared that she had done something wrong and he wasn't telling her. Her feelings were hurt. She let me know that there had been a shift in Phil's behavior a few weeks ago, and he was becoming more and more distant. He wasn't as attentive during their times together, would forget to call when he said he would, and had canceled their last date minutes before they were supposed to meet and didn't even apologize. She couldn't wrap her head around what was happening and couldn't imagine treating someone like that. His behavior felt rude and cruel to her, and she was ready to end things immediately.

In any relationship, there is a learning curve as you get to know the other person. The change in Phil felt so sudden and out of character that Barbara didn't know what to do. First, we went through a grounding exercise and meditation to get her centered and calm her nervous system. Then we began to process the feelings around the subject. She was feeling a confusing mix of anger and sadness, and I could tell that she was placing judgment on both feelings. I acknowledged her feelings and acknowledged and validated her emotional experience. I told her that given everything that was happening, her feelings made sense and she was justified in feeling them. As we discussed the impulses to action or what these feelings were making her want to do, she spoke about wanting to confront Phil to ask why he was behaving like this and find out if she had done something to make him behave this way. And part of her wanted to run and avoid the whole thing, to avoid the hurt and call it quits immediately. From the calmer space she was in now, she knew neither of these options was in their best interests at the moment. Noting the options helped us to uncover more about how she viewed the situation and where her judgments and perspective were now. From there we could start to explore empathy as a way to gain perspective and insight into how to move forward in a way that honored Barbara and Phil's connection.

I asked Barbara what she wanted from our session together. She said she wanted to have a clearer understanding of the situation and to let go of the fear and resentment that she was feeling toward Phil.

Empathetic Inquiry

Developing empathy is a major focus of the work that I do with clients. I've found that a mindful and compassionate approach that allows for a full understanding of another's worldview can help strengthen people's ability to cultivate presence, enhance their emotional awareness, and foster connection in their relationships. By moving through a process of Empathetic Inquiry, people can gain insight into the other person's perspective and see the situation more holistically.

Once Barbara was in a calm space, I led her through a series of questions that would help her begin to put her own worldview aside and see the situation through Phil's eyes. This practice is never intended to excuse behaviors or to bypass the communication that needs to take place, but it can be helpful in alleviating the fear and resentment you may be holding on to. Barbara had mentioned that doing so was her goal.

First, I had Barbara put herself in Phil's shoes and describe to me why he was behaving as he was. She thought for a moment and then went into a long explanation of all the things that she had done to upset him. She said she was being too clingy and that he had decided that a relationship wasn't worth his time. Rather than having that conversation with her, he was simply distancing himself until she got the point.

This was a perfect example of how sometimes we think we are extending empathy and understanding by putting ourselves in the other's shoes but our own worldview is getting in the way and showing us the situation through our own filter. In this case, I asked Barabara another one of my favorite questions: "How true is it that Phil thinks that you're too clingy and not worth his time, and what is the evidence you have to support that?" She admitted that he had never said or alluded to any of that. This was most likely an example of her gremlin voice (Chapter 5) showing up and clouding her judgment.

With the awareness of her skewed perspective, I asked if she would be willing to go through a series of questions that might help her understand Phil's perspective. I told her that she may not know the answer to some of the questions but that she should answer them to the best of her knowledge. She agreed, and we went through the Empathetic Inquiry questions one at a time.

What Values and Beliefs May Be Guiding Phil's Actions?

In the months that she had spent getting to know Phil, Barbara had grown to understand his deep commitment to his faith, how much he valued loyalty and respect, and how his family was a top priority to him. It was important to him to always honor his late wife and keep her memory alive for his children and grandchildren. These values clearly sat at the center of his decision making and undoubtedly would guide him as he developed his relationship with Barbara.

What Life Experiences and Background May Have Influenced His Perspective?

Barbara knew that Phil's relationship with his late wife had shaped his life in many ways. She was reminded of the openness and honesty they shared in discussing their partners. While they were forging a new relationship, they both agreed that there would be no replacing the connections they once had. The loss of his wife deeply affected Phil, and that experience of love and loss would certainly influence his perspective on dating, especially as things became more serious.

How May Phil's Actions Have Benefited Him?

This is one of the more difficult questions that I asked, and it required Barbara to fully step out of her own perspective and look at the situation through Phil's eyes. When she did, she could see that even though Phil's actions were causing emotional distance in their relationship, they might be providing him with a sense of comfort and familiarity in his grief, allowing him to navigate emotions authentically and honor his wife. It makes sense that experiencing joyful moments of connection while attempting to grieve would be conflicting and painful. Putting a momentary pause on his growing relationship with Barbara might be serving as a way of protecting himself.

Why Would His Actions Make Perfect Sense for Him?

This is my favorite question. Barbara sat with it for a moment and then remembered that the anniversary of Phil's wife's passing happened around the time when he started to pull away. It had just been three years now. His deep love and commitment to his late wife clearly were impacting how he was able to show up in his relationship with Barbara. It made sense that he would pull away and temporarily distance himself from Barbara in order to protect himself and process his grief.

Barbara realized that while she had been without her husband for a decade, the situation was much fresher for Phil, and it made sense that he'd be confused and in pain and want to pull away. She remembered her experience of loss and how long it had taken, and how many years of therapy and coaching, until she had gotten to the point she was at. She had been looking at this situation entirely from her own perspective. Now she recognized that other possibilities exist besides the narrative she had crafted in her mind.

Without a deeper discussion with Phil, all of this was speculation, of course, but this exercise allowed Barbara to begin to recognize another perspective and extend empathy and understanding to Phil. And from a space of nonjudgement and openness, we looked at the final question.

What Is the Pain Underneath All of This, and How Can You Show Compassion to Help Alleviate Their Suffering?

Given what she had realized through these questions, it was clear that Phil was still grieving the loss of his wife. Regardless of his reasons for pulling away, Barbara needed to be there to extend her support and compassion. She knew firsthand the experience of seeing those first few years roll by and the experience of *saudade* that existed while she learned to live without her husband by her side. She needed to be there for Phil.

Building Connection

The following week, Barbara told me that she had had a chance to meet with Phil. From an open and nonjudgmental space, she brought up what she had discovered in our session. She let him know that she noticed that there had been a shift in how he was showing up in their relationship, and she wanted to check in with him. Initially he was uncertain about what was going on with him and told Barbara that it truly had nothing to do with her; he was simply feeling lost and confused, and the only thing he knew to do was pull away so he wouldn't place the burden of his confusing emotions on her.

Barbara told Phil about the Empathetic Inquiry questions that she had done in her session and some of the things that came up for her. It turned out to be a great tool for Phil as well, and she guided him through them so he could gain a clearer understanding of what he was facing and more accurately articulate to her what was happening. In the end, they developed a deeper sense of empathy for each other and themselves and were able to support one another and show up with compassion and care.

The Process of Understanding Empathy

Use the Empathetic Inquiry process when you are trying to deepen your understanding of a person in your life and to show up with empathy and compassion. Whether it's a friend, colleague, family member, or an intimate partner, this process can guide you. And just as Phil realized, it is also a beneficial tool when you need to develop a sense of self-empathy and further understand yourself and why you are showing up the way you are.

Step 1: What Values and Beliefs May Be Guiding Their Actions and Decisions?

Explore the core values and beliefs that shape a person's behavior and choices. Understanding their underlying principles can provide insight into their motivations and perspective.

Example: Phil's pulling away and becoming distant in his new relationship may be driven by deep love and commitment to his late wife. He may be prioritizing honoring their history, even if it means temporarily distancing himself from others.

Step 2: What Life Experiences and Background May Have Influenced Their Perspective?

Reflect on a person's life experiences and background to gain a deeper understanding of their worldview. Past experiences shape perceptions and influence attitudes and behaviors.

Example: Phil's past experiences of love, loss, and commitment, combined with family dynamics, may significantly influence his perspective on relationships and grieving, leading to actions that seem distant or withdrawn to others.

Step 3: How May Their Actions or Beliefs Benefit Them?

Consider the positive aspects or benefits that a person derives from their actions or beliefs. Recognizing the value they see in their choices can foster empathy and understanding.

Example: Despite causing emotional distance in a current relationship, Phil's actions may provide him with a sense of comfort and familiarity in his grief, allowing him to navigate emotions authentically and to honor his past relationship.

Step 4: What May Support Their Beliefs?

Identify the sources of validation or reinforcement that support a person's beliefs. Understanding these influences can provide context for their worldview.

Example: Phil may find support and validation for his beliefs from his children that prioritize honoring the relationship with their mother or navigating grief in a particular way, shaping his actions and choices.

Step 5: Why Would This Decision or Belief Make Perfect Sense for Them?

Consider why a person's decision or beliefs align with their unique circumstances, values, and experiences. Recognizing the rationale behind their choices can foster empathy and compassion.

Example: Given Phil's deep love and commitment to his late wife and the possible pressure from his children, it makes sense for him to prioritize honoring that history, even if it means temporarily distancing himself from a new relationship. His decision may be driven by a genuine desire to navigate grief in a way that feels authentic and respectful.

Step 6: What Is the Possible Pain Underneath Their Actions and Decisions, and How Can Others Show Compassion and Help to Alleviate Their Suffering?

Explore the underlying emotions or struggles that may contribute to a person's behavior or beliefs. Recognizing their pain allows you to extend compassion and support.

Example: Phil may be experiencing profound feelings of sadness, guilt, and confusion as he navigates grief and adjusts to life without his late wife. Barbara can show compassion by listening empathically, validating his emotions, and offering reassurance and comfort during this challenging time. By demonstrating patience, understanding, and unconditional support, listeners can help him feel seen, heard, and loved as he works through his grief and begins to heal.

Calm Kit Tool #8: Nonjudgment Practice

Nonjudgment Practice in mindfulness involves observing your thoughts, emotions, and experiences without evaluating them as good or bad, right or wrong. It's about cultivating a stance of open curiosity and acceptance toward whatever arises in your awareness, without getting caught up in judgments or criticisms. Here's an exercise to practice nonjudgment in mindfulness.

1. **Settle into a comfortable position.** Find a quiet and comfortable space where you can sit or lie down without distractions. Close your eyes if it feels comfortable, or maintain a soft gaze.
2. **Bring awareness to your breath.** Begin by bringing your attention to your breath. Notice the sensation of each inhale and exhale, feeling the rhythm of your breath as it flows in and out of your body.
3. **Observe your thoughts.** As you continue to focus on your breath, allow your thoughts to come and go without trying to control or suppress them. Notice any thoughts that arise in your mind, whether they're positive or negative, pleasant or unpleasant.
4. **Practice nonjudgment.** As you observe your thoughts, practice nonjudgment by simply noticing them without

getting caught up in them. Instead of labeling your thoughts as good or bad, right or wrong, simply acknowledge them with curiosity and acceptance.

5. **Notice your emotions.** Along with your thoughts, pay attention to any emotions or feelings that arise within you. Allow yourself to experience these emotions without judgment, simply observing them with an attitude of openness and acceptance.

6. **Bring compassion to your experience.** If you notice any judgments or criticisms arising, gently redirect your attention back to your breath and the present moment. Offer yourself compassion and understanding for any judgments that arise, reminding yourself that it's natural for the mind to judge and that you can choose to let go of these judgments.

7. **Return to the present moment.** Throughout the practice, continually bring your attention back to the present moment whenever you notice your mind wandering or getting caught up in judgments. Use your breath as an anchor to ground yourself in the here and now.

8. **Reflect on your experience.** After you've practiced for a few minutes, take a moment to reflect on your experience. Notice how it felt to observe your thoughts and emotions without judgment. Reflect on any insights or observations that arose during the practice.

9. **Integrate nonjudgment into daily life.** As you go about your day, continue to practice nonjudgment in your interactions and experiences. Notice any judgments that arise, and practice letting them go with compassion and acceptance. Cultivate a stance of openness and curiosity toward yourself and others, allowing for greater peace and understanding in your life.

Practicing nonjudgment in mindfulness allows you to cultivate greater self-awareness, acceptance, and compassion toward yourself and others. By observing your thoughts and experiences without judgment, you can cultivate a deeper sense of inner peace and well-being in your life.

11 Navigating Anger

A Gentle Reminder

As you navigate through difficult emotional experiences in life, it's important to remember that there are no good or bad emotions. It's easy to associate the feelings of joy and happiness with "good" and anger or sadness with "bad," but each feeling serves a purpose and is neutral in nature. Emotions serve as messengers, signaling your needs, desires, and boundaries. They offer insights into your values, beliefs, and experiences, guiding you in navigating the complexities of life. Instead of labeling emotions as "good" or "bad," begin to embrace them as natural and valid responses to your circumstances and indicators that something needs to be addressed.

Anger is an uncomfortable emotion as it elicits such strong reactions to the situation at hand, but

(continued)

just because something is uncomfortable doesn't mean that it is bad. There are lessons to be learned from anger. When you learn to allow anger to be present in your life, you open yourself to fuller experiences.

Anger can be a perfectly justifiable response to what is occurring in life. It can also be an overactive measure of protection that causes us to leap into action before taking time to assess the situation. Anger, just like all emotions, is not inherently bad, but when unchecked and unharnessed, it can create situations in which we act aggressively and without consideration for others. Most likely we all have been on the receiving end of anger and felt discomfort and fear in the face of someone who seems to have lost control. We've also most likely all been in situations where a sense of anger builds within and we express it forcefully toward someone. Because of these experiences, we may view anger as a violent, painful emotion that tears relationships apart. Perceiving anger as a monster to be feared causes us to avoid it by either suppressing it or running from situations that could potentially cause anger.

Anger, however, can exist as a healthy response to indicate that a fight is necessary. Anger is required to fight injustice and motivate us to stand for what is right. It can lead us to engage in conversations that need to be held and to improve our relationships by moving us away from unspoken resentments. Anger also can be a signal that we need to address a deeper unfelt emotion, like sadness, shame, inadequacy, or hopelessness. By approaching anger with curiosity, we can strengthen our emotional intelligence and gain a deeper understanding of our emotions and triggers.

Although avoiding anger often is unhealthier than expressing it, most people are not taught how to process or express anger. Through mindfulness, we can carefully draw awareness to our emotional experiences in the present moment and can, with curiosity and care, begin to determine how we want to respond. Anger comes from an activation of the sympathetic nervous system and is the fight part of the fight-or-flight response. That anger response leads us to take quick action to avoid a perceived threat. It's a valuable tool when we are being chased by a bear in the wilderness, but it's not as useful when someone bumps into us in line at the grocery store. By using mindfulness to develop a conscious awareness of thought, feeling, and the impulses to action when anger arises, we can pause for a moment and assess the situation before taking direct action. A mindful approach to anger allows us to take control of our emotions and align our actions with how we want to be in the world.

Anger is a typical part of the human condition, and from time to time we all experience moments of anger. When the severity and frequency of that anger contributes to issues with relationships, work performance, and mental health, it is best to be worked through with a mental health provider. Such anger may be part of a larger mental health condition, such as intermittent explosive disorder, oppositional defiant disorder, or even depression.

Creating a healthy relationship with anger and learning how to express it in a healthy manner will improve many areas of life including self-awareness, mental health, and physical health, and will strengthen relationships with others. Learning how to work through your anger in a healthy manner can be difficult, but as with most things in life, the first step is awareness.

Unharnessed Anger

Ethan was a corporate client sent to me by his CEO after a disastrous 360 review conducted by his company. This assessment was intended to gauge employees' leadership qualities, interpersonal skills, efficiency, and problem-solving ability. His colleagues, direct reports, managers, had completed the assessment, and the results were compared to his assessment of himself. Prior to our first session together, I spoke with the CEO about the results. While it was clear that Ethan was recognized for his work performance and ability to perform his role, his interpersonal skills and leadership qualities were sorely lacking. Everyone who filled out the assessment mentioned his inability to control his temper—everyone but Ethan. There was a major disconnect between Ethan's awareness of how he was showing up at work and what others were experiencing. Ethan had given himself the highest marks in terms of interpersonal skills. The only mention of the anger that everyone else spoke about was a comment that he felt he was able to keep calm under pressure.

When meeting with people who do not come for coaching voluntarily, it's difficult to gauge a client's level of interest. Ethan was mandated to attend sessions with me by his company. Sometimes in these situations we are a great fit and the benefits of coaching are seen immediately; other times clients are counting the minutes waiting for the session to end so they can check it off their agenda for the day.

Ethan was a clock watcher. Not only that, he had a terrible habit of checking his emails during our sessions, which took place via Zoom. He attempted to place his phone directly off camera so I couldn't see it in the frame of his video. Obviously he believed I wasn't aware that he was actively keeping tabs on work during our sessions. His expressive eyes, however, made it abundantly clear that he was distracted. At least five times through our 45-minute sessions I'd watch him reach over, open an email, get red, and tense up, all while he was pretending to be connected to the conversation we were having.

I let the situation slide for a few weeks, but eventually, when we were both more comfortable with each other, I asked what he was feeling when those emails came through. It was a good opportunity to begin to draw Ethan's awareness to the physical sensations present when something triggered him. Without judgment or shame, I let him know that I noticed that occasionally when he looked down and to the right, his face would get red and his shoulders would tighten. Initially he tried to deny it and say that everything was fine, but after a few moments, he went into a tirade about how incompetent his team was and how they were always asking him the most ridiculous questions. I encouraged him to let himself feel that anger and continue to speak. As he continued to rant, I noted that sweat started to pool above his brow, and I could physically see his body getting hotter. His face flushed red as he pulled on his tie to loosen the top button of his collar. His body was tensing, and he was slowly tearing to pieces the piece of paper that was in his hands. After a few moments, he dropped his face into his hands and started to massage the bridge of his nose as a way to relieve the sinus pressure that was clearly present for him.

When things started to settle, I asked Ethan to explain what he had felt and if that was a common occurrence for him. Interestingly, his experience was much different from what I had observed. To him, this was just a normal conversation about work. He didn't feel it was heightened, and in his mind he was just letting me know what was going on with the email he had just read. The results of the 360 review made a lot more sense to me now. Obviously there was a major disconnect between what he was projecting and his awareness of himself. Without a sense of awareness, he was never going to be able to understand the impact of his words and actions on those around him.

Recognizing Anger

Over the next few weeks, I worked with Ethan on cultivating awareness of his thoughts, feelings, and instincts to action through a series of mindfulness-based exercises. Initially, he wasn't interested in meditation, but when I introduced him to some of the scientific research on mindfulness and explained the documented benefits on individual performance, he was willing to try a few exercises.

We started by working through basic grounding techniques and practices in each session. Now during our sessions, I encouraged him to keep his email open. When he received an email that started to elicit a strong response, I let him get to a point where the physical manifestations of anger were becoming apparent, and then I asked him to move through a Body Scan and begin to explain what he was feeling as he reached each part of the body. He would note the sinus pressure, the sweat on his forehead, the tightness in his chest, and the feeling of heat within his stomach. We'd then debrief and talk about how he could use awareness of those physical symptoms as indicators that he was experiencing an intense emotion.

Another exercise that we explored in sessions was a journaling exercise to help identify thoughts as they arose in real time. When Ethan began to feel a sense of anger, as identified by the physical symptoms we had discussed, I'd have him free write the thoughts that were present for him. I directed him to let every thought that entered his mind flow freely onto the page without judgment or the need to censor anything. Afterward he read them back and determined which thoughts were beneficial to the situation and which were intensified by anger. He found that many of the thoughts that determined his actions were overreactions to the current situation. Without awareness, he was allowing those thoughts to determine his actions and not pausing to determine if they were the right size for the circumstances.

It's amazing how often we are convinced that our decisions are justified and in our best interest without considering the reality of the situation. Remember that, as humans, we are comfort-seeking machines. Anger is a difficult emotion that causes a great deal of discomfort, so it makes sense that we want to move away from it quickly. When our sympathetic nervous system is activated in moments of anger, we want to fight to get away from the sensations we're experiencing. Without awareness, we continue to be led by these instincts. Then afterward we are left to deal with broken lives. The practice of mindful awareness allows us to notice the entirety of a situation and to pause for a moment, long enough to determine if the action that we're about to take aligns with how we want to show up in the world.

Clarifying Intentions

Once Ethan was more comfortable drawing awareness to the thoughts, physical sensations, and impulses to action that were present for him in moments of anger, we were able to start to explore the actions that he was taking at work when he was angry and see if they were aligned with who he wanted to be as a leader in the company. When I reviewed his 360 assessment from others, I noted that many people said that Ethan was abrasive; one even went as far as to say he was abusive. In contrast, Ethan saw himself as decisive, supportive, and passionate.

I asked him to tell me more about terms he had used to describe himself and to give me a picture of how he wanted to be perceived by his coworkers. He was very clear about the type of boss he wanted to be. He wanted to show up as kind yet firm and be someone who was there to help others find the quickest solution to any problem. He wanted to motivate and support the people he managed and be perceived as someone whose passion led him to excel in everything that he did.

What did Ethan think about the fact that his colleagues had such a different view of him? When I asked about it, he said that it was something that he'd dealt with his entire life. He had felt misunderstood since he was a kid and believed that people often mistook his directness for rudeness. It had cost him friendships, relationships, and even jobs in the past. Clearly his anger and lack of awareness were causing a great deal of distress in his life, but instead of addressing it long ago, he had convinced himself that *other* people were the problem, which fueled his quickness to anger even more.

I sensed that we needed to do two things to help Ethan navigate through his anger:

1. We needed to continue to have him become aware of his anger and be able to recognize when that anger was present.
2. We needed Ethan to gain the ability to pause before acting and to sit with anger for a moment.

Allowing Anger

It's important to be open to everything that we feel and not deceive ourselves by ignoring parts that we would rather not experience. Often when we are faced with a difficult emotion, we suppress it and bury it deep within, move to rid ourselves of the emotion in the quickest way possible, or convince ourselves that it's actually something else entirely. We would rather live in denial than deal with the issue. We need to allow anger so we can come to a place where we can fully feel and examine that anger, and then we can allow it to pass.

There is, however, a difference between allowing anger and venting anger. Allowing anger is permitting the natural response to a perceived threat, injustice, or frustration to be present. When we feel anger, our bodies may respond with physiological changes, such as increased heart rate, muscle tension, and adrenaline release as well as racing thoughts, all preparing us for action. In allowing it to be present, we're drawing full awareness to these changes and investigating the circumstances so we can recognize any perceived threat. Sitting with anger also allows us to begin to identify emotions that may be lying beneath the anger and triggering it.

Venting anger, in contrast, involves expressing or releasing pent-up feelings verbally or physically by yelling, screaming, slamming doors, or engaging in aggressive behavior. Venting anger is often seen as a way to "let off steam" or release built-up tension. However, while venting may provide temporary relief, it can also have negative consequences. Venting anger can escalate conflicts, damage relationships, and reinforce negative patterns of behavior. It may alienate others, create feelings of fear or resentment, and lead to further misunderstandings. Additionally, venting anger can perpetuate a cycle of anger and aggression, as it fails to address the underlying issues that triggered the emotion in the first place.

Ethan had become an expert at venting anger, so much so that his outbursts felt like normal communication to him. By venting his anger so readily, he had created a default method of responding to situations that triggered anger; the method felt natural to him but created negative consequences all around him. What he was not equipped to do was allow anger to be present without taking immediate action.

We had already begun the initial work of strengthening his ability to recognize anger and draw awareness to the physiological and mental changes that occurred in the face of anger as well as the impulses to action. The next thing we focused on was permitting those feelings to stay and allowing the discomfort to be present for a while.

Because Ethan was always in action and always felt the need to be doing something, slowing down to allow discomfort to be present was not something he enjoyed. During our sessions, we worked on slowing his mind and body by focusing on his breath and returning to the awareness of the inhale and exhale in when he felt his anger rise. I'd ask him simply to narrate his experience to me rather than leaping into action, all the while continuing to come back to the breath. His first few attempts ended with him directing his anger at me and escaping it by calling me a host of names. But eventually he could feel the anger and allow it to be there without needing to jump into action.

During one of our sessions, Ethan received a message from a client letting him know that they were incredibly disappointed by the meeting they had had earlier that morning. They mentioned that they felt he and his team were unprepared and sloppy, and they were strongly considering ending their contract. Understandably, this caused Ethan a great deal of distress, and as his anger began to rise, I asked him to narrate the experience. He walked me through the physical sensations he was experiencing and noted those same telltale signs he'd witnessed before. His body temperature was rising, his face was starting to flush, and he could physically feel his heartbeat quickening in his chest. Then he started narrating the thoughts that were swirling around in his head. It would vacillate from his gremlin voice (Chapter 5) telling him how terrible he was at his job and what an idiot he was to thoughts of how unfair he was being treated by the client. Then he was up on his feet and describing his thoughts of attacking the client, insulting everything from his appearance to his job performance. It was clear that Ethan's anger was rising, and he was searching for somewhere to place it besides within himself.

After Ethan had a chance to narrate his experience, I asked him what it would feel like to allow those feelings to stay for a minute without needing to take action. He sat back down and let things be. I could sense him wanting to pick up his phone to email or call to speak his mind, but he let himself take a few moments and concentrate on the awareness of the inhale through the nose and exhale through the mouth. Within a few seconds of simply allowing himself to be with his anger, he burst into tears.

Investigating Anger

This was the first time I had ever seen Ethan get to the point of tears, and I held space for him as he navigated his way through the experience. By allowing the anger to be present for him, he had begun to feel the emotions that were beneath that anger. Those deeper emotions that his gremlin voice was trying to protect him from having to feel were coming to the surface, and for the first time in a long while, he was allowing himself to be with them.

After a few moments, he started to tell me that he felt a lot of shame and embarrassment that he had been called out in an email with his boss copied. He felt sad that he was portrayed in a light that was so far from what he thought of himself. He also felt frustrated that he had put so much work and care into preparing for the presentation and it was perceived as a failure.

Slowly, as he let himself investigate what was behind the anger, I asked him to return his awareness to his body and start to note the physical sensations that were present for him now. The tension, tightness, and heat of anger had slowly started to move away, replaced with a heaviness of the body as he let himself feel into the sadness that existed beneath the anger. Then I asked him what his impulse to do at that moment was. Before he wanted to pick up the phone and have his voice be heard; now, allowing for this sadness to be present, he just wanted to be there for a minute and not deal with anything. We sat for a moment and then decided what his best next step would be.

Deciding What's Best

It's not that one emotion is better than another or that allowing anger to be present is inherently wrong; it's that the intensity of anger can be so jarring that it forces quick action without thought. At the same time, heavier emotions like sadness can cause a freeze response that prevents us from taking action. In both scenarios, if we were to move based on our initial instinct to action, likely we would not end up where we truly want to be. After you've allowed yourself to experience anger and investigate it, it's important to take a mindful pause and determine what action aligns with your values and focuses on resolution rather than escalation.

I sat with Ethan for a moment as he tried to decide how he wanted to move forward. I went back to the intentions that we had spoken about several weeks ago and reminded him that his intention was to show up at work as someone who was decisive, supportive, and passionate. I asked him to look at the situation from that perspective and see what options might best align with that. He could act in several ways. He could lead with his initial instinct and have a forceful phone conversation, letting his client know how wrong he was; he could call his entire team into his office and let them know how disappointed he was in them; he could choose to do nothing and avoid the situation entirely; or he could allow the dust to settle and have a conversation with his team about what the best next steps would be, so together they could make the best decision.

Ethan knew what the right answer was. From a calm and centered space, he put a meeting for his team on the calendar for the next day. It was an opportunity for him to show his passion for the work they do; to collaborate and be open to feedback; and to come up with a decisive solution to the problem. It was fully in alignment with who he wanted to be, and it let him move through anger and toward a resolution.

Six months after our first session, I discussed Ethan's progress with the CEO of the company. I was pleased with the work he was doing during our sessions, but I never can be sure of the impact it was having on his coworkers. The CEO said that the experience had been really positive, and watching Ethan pause and count his breaths instead of shouting in company meetings was a very welcome sight. The anger was still going to be there, but Ethan had a few new tools to help him gain control over it, and he had become the passionate leader he wanted to be.

The Process of Navigating Anger

Navigating anger is a challenging yet essential aspect of emotional well-being. In the face of life's challenges, understanding and managing anger can lead to healthier relationships, improved communication, and personal growth. By cultivating mindful awareness, clarifying personal intentions, and exploring the underlying emotions behind anger, individuals can learn to respond to anger in constructive ways that align with their values and promote positive outcomes. Through self-reflection, practice, and, when needed, professional support, individuals can develop the skills they need to navigate anger with resilience and compassion.

Step 1: Recognize the Nature of Anger

Acknowledge that emotions, including anger, serve as messengers, signaling needs, desires, and boundaries. Embrace the idea that all emotions are natural responses to circumstances and hold valuable insights into personal values and beliefs.

Step 2: Understand Anger's Purpose

Recognize anger as a justifiable response to situations but understand its potential to become overactive. Appreciate anger's role in addressing injustice, setting boundaries, and uncovering deeper, unfelt emotions, such as sadness or shame.

Step 3: Cultivate Mindful Awareness

Develop mindfulness practices to assess situations before reacting impulsively. Learn to recognize how the body responds in moments of anger, such as increased heart rate or muscle tension, and navigate those responses consciously, allowing for a moment of pause and reflection before responding.

Step 4: Develop Awareness of Anger Triggers

Identify specific situations, thoughts, or actions that trigger feelings of anger. Practice observing physical and emotional responses to these triggers without judgment, allowing for a deeper understanding of the underlying causes of anger.

Step 5: Practice Emotional Regulation Techniques

Engage in grounding techniques and mindfulness practices to manage intense emotions in the moment. Experiment with journaling to identify and challenge thoughts intensified by anger, fostering a greater sense of emotional regulation and self-awareness.

Step 6: Clarify Personal Intentions

Reflect on personal values and goals in various situations where anger arises. Consider how actions aligned with these values can lead to desired outcomes and perceptions, promoting healthier responses to anger-inducing situations.

Step 7: Allow the Experience of Anger

Distinguish between allowing anger to be present and venting anger destructively. Practice sitting with anger and observing it without reacting impulsively, allowing you to acknowledge and explore the discomfort of anger without immediately seeking resolution.

Step 8: Investigate Underlying Emotions

Explore deeper emotions masked by anger, using mindfulness techniques to observe physical sensations and thoughts associated with these underlying feelings. Allow space for these emotions to be fully felt and understood.

Step 9: Decide on Constructive Actions

Pause mindfully before taking action in response to anger, considering how actions align with personal values and intentions. Choose actions that promote understanding, collaboration, and resolution in relationships and work environments rather than escalating conflicts.

Step 10: Monitor Progress and Seek Support

Reflect on the effectiveness of coping strategies and emotional regulation techniques over time. Seek feedback from trusted individuals and professionals to gauge your progress in managing anger, and continue prioritizing self-awareness and personal growth in navigating emotions. Also remember to gauge the severity of anger when it begins to impact relationships or mental health. Consider seeking support from a mental health provider to address underlying conditions or patterns of behavior that contribute to anger.

Calm Kit Tool #9: Anger RAID Meditation

Navigating anger can be challenging, but by practicing the Anger RAID Meditation, you can approach this emotion with greater awareness and understanding. The Anger RAID Meditation involves recognizing, allowing, investigating, and determining next steps when you experience anger. A meditation script can be found in Chapter 14. Here's an explanation of the four-step process included in the meditation:

1. **Recognize anger.** The first step in navigating anger is to recognize when it arises within you. Doing this involves tuning in to your body and mind to identify the physical sensations, thoughts, and emotions associated with anger. Pay attention to physical signs, such as increased heart rate, muscle tension, and clenched jaw, and to racing thoughts or feelings of irritation or frustration.

2. **Allow anger to be present.** Once you've recognized that you're experiencing anger, the next step is to allow yourself to fully experience it without judgment or resistance. Doing this means acknowledging the presence of anger without trying to suppress, deny, or escalate it. Allow yourself to sit with the discomfort of anger and observe it with an attitude of openness and acceptance.

3. **Investigate the root cause.** With mindfulness, explore the underlying causes and triggers of your anger. Reflect on what specific thoughts, beliefs, or external events may have contributed to its emergence. Investigate whether any unmet needs, past experiences, or habitual patterns are fueling your anger. By examining the root cause of your anger, you can gain insight into its origins and better understand why it has arisen in this moment.

4. **Determine next steps.** After recognizing, allowing, and investigating your anger, determine the most appropriate next steps to take. Doing this may involve choosing how to respond to the situation or deciding whether action is necessary. Consider whether expressing your anger directly, setting boundaries, seeking support, or practicing self-care would be the most effective way to address it. Choose responses that align with your values and support your well-being and the well-being of others involved.

12 Leading with Love

A Gentle Reminder

One of the most powerful moments in life is when you discover that you do not need to be fully healed in order to experience love and that even in your brokenness you are worthy of receiving and capable of giving loving-kindness. When you can stop waiting for healing to be complete to enjoy life, you open yourself up to experience the beauty of the present moment in its entirety. Instead of seeing healing as a destination to reach before you can open yourself up to the love that exists, you begin to see that you are worthy of those experiences right here, right now. As you embrace your brokenness and vulnerabilities, you find a deeper sense of love for yourself and for others.

After I sat through my first Loving-Kindness (Metta) Meditation, when I opened my eyes, I saw an entire studio of people who looked deeply moved, many with tears rolling down their faces. There was a discussion afterward, and people shared the transformative power of the meditation. They explained how it had deepened their relationships, allowed them to gain an awareness of what it felt like to experience love and be able to share it, and how each time they practiced it, they felt they were able to let go of pain that existed in old relationships and lean in with love.

I sat there confused, wondering what meditation they had just sat through. For me, it was some cheesy nonsense that took too long and caused my mind to wander in a million directions. I fully admit that I was judging every minute of the meditation. I was clearly not a fan and definitely didn't plan on adding it to my repertoire of meditations.

Understanding Loving-Kindness

In the meditative practice of loving-kindness, or *metta* (from the Pāli language), the object of attention and awareness focuses on silent phrases that serve as wishes for peace, health, and prosperity. The intention is to shift our default mode of thinking, which tends to be negative, toward a kinder and gentler tone. In the practice of loving-kindness, those silent phrases are extended to different sets of people in our lives. Loving-kindness phrases are simple and organic so that the experience occurs naturally within you. They can be any phrases that resonate with you, but the traditional phrases are wishes for yourself and others to feel safe and well within their minds, bodies, and the world and to experience positive emotions and ease. Examples include

- May you be happy.
- May you be healthy.
- May you be safe.
- May you live with ease.

Once you have chosen a set of phrases that resonate with you, silently extend those phrases to different people in your life. These phrases can change or remain the same over time, and no set number of phrases is needed. What is important is that the intention of the phrases resonates with you. Begin first with an extension of loving-kindness to yourself, then to a loved one, then to a neutral person, then to someone with whom you've had conflict, and then to the world around you. Change the phrasing depending on whom you are referencing, beginning each phrase with "May I," "May you," or "May all beings."

The traditional Buddhist practice of loving-kindness has been around for thousands of years. It has been praised by researchers as a way to increase positive emotions and decrease negative ones; to increase vagal tone, which increases social connection and positivity; and even to decrease symptoms of posttraumatic stress disorder, chronic pain, and migraines.

I had read amazing studies about the power of loving-kindness, yet after the practice I was sitting in a meditation room wanting to crawl out of my skin. However, I had experienced the benefits of other types of meditation and understood that the consistency of daily practice was what produced results, so I placed my judgment aside. According to most of the studies I had read, seven weeks of practicing loving-kindness daily was enough time to see improvement, so I committed to adding Loving-Kindness (Metta) Meditation to my daily practice for seven weeks.

Concentrated Effort

When I first started working out, my trainer told me that to make progress, you don't need to be extreme; you just need to be consistent. As someone who had always been all or nothing, this was tough for me, but over time the results did come, and it was the consistency that came from manageable routines that led me there. When I started to create my meditation practice, I forgot that valuable information. To get the result I wanted, I thought I had to do silent meditation retreats once a month and set aside hours and hours of time to be in stillness each day. But what actually was most beneficial was creating simple daily habits of mindfulness that would remind me to come back to center and ground myself in the present moment.

One of the daily habits that I added to my morning and evening routines was loving-kindness. At the end of my meditation, I would go through the phrases that I felt most connected to and direct them to myself and others in my life. They were

- May you be held in loving-kindness.
- May you feel joy without pain.
- May you feel protected and peaceful.
- May you feel connected and calm.
- May you be well.

Noticing Changes

I spent the next few weeks consistently practicing loving-kindness each morning and evening. After three weeks of devoted effort, the practice still felt mechanical and dry. I was feeling restless and even experiencing heightened emotions like anger and grief during the meditation. Luckily, I'm a very stubborn man and had committed to seven weeks of consistency, so I pushed through.

During the seventh week of practice, I sat down and started to look at my life to see if anything had shifted since I started my Loving-Kindness Meditations. I knew that I had grown to enjoy the consistency of the phrases as bookends for the day, but wanted to take stock of the different areas of my life. I took out my journal and wrote down each of the sets of people that loving-kindness is directed to: Self, Loved Ones, Neutral People, People with Whom I'm in Conflict, and the World Around Me. I took time to write about what I'd discovered and what shifted for me over the past few weeks. In stepping back, I realized that quite a bit had changed and that maybe I had been a bit quick to judge the practice during my first session.

Directing Loving-Kindness Inward

Directing loving-kindness to myself was probably the most difficult of all at first. I'd close my eyes and begin to say the words, and my gremlin voice (Chapter 5) would come out screaming that it was ridiculous. I'd find myself in a battle between drawing my awareness to the phrases and attempting to silence the gremlin. Eventually, over the weeks, I did note that he quieted down, and I would feel more connected.

Most notably, for the first time, I started to feel a sense of endearment and care being directed inward similar to that which I shared so easily with my loved ones. If the self-love visualization helped me to find the right words to say to begin to experience a sense of self-love, the Loving-Kindness Meditation gave me the physical and emotional connection to self-love that I had been searching for.

Connecting with Loved Ones

The practice of connecting with loved ones came easily to me. It was easy to maintain focus on the phrases when they were directed toward someone I truly cared about. I could imagine their faces and connect with them as if they were sitting right in front of me. Emotional moments arose from the memories that came from imagining their faces, but I never tried to run from the emotions. I also noticed that I was beginning to reach out and share that love in real life more often. I have always had an aversion to speaking on the phone, but I found myself calling people just to let them know I was thinking of them and wanted to send love their way.

Recognizing the Humanity in All People

I was surprised to find that I was starting to connect more with those neutral people in my life. Although I recognized the doorman or the person who worked in the deli, I didn't really have an understanding of many of the people who served important functions in my life. I didn't know their names and didn't even think to wonder where they lived. But in spending the past few weeks sending well wishes to them,

I suddenly began to see them in a new way. So often we tend to look through people we don't know, but loving-kindness changes that pattern and gives us the ability to see people and recognize their humanity.

Reassessing Conflict with Others

I also noticed a shift in the way that I was relating to the people in my life with whom I'd had conflict. I've never been great at expressing anger. In my attempts to avoid conflict, I have a habit of jumping to a resolution and letting people off the hook, even when they've hurt me. Initially I didn't think I was actively in conflict with anyone in my life. During the meditation, I thought back to the kids who bullied me in high school and directed the phrase to them. Doing so felt fine and helped to release some of the pain I still might have been carrying. This was the part of the meditation where I'd begin to sense anger and grief coming up, and I couldn't figure out why.

During that time, my mind would also go to sad and anger-filled memories of my mom leaving home, or my dad saying something incredibly hurtful, or the times I had my heart broken again and again in college. While I thought that I had moved past these moments and wasn't carrying resentment, clearly I was. As my heart began to soften by the ongoing extension of love, it was revealing the pain that was held beneath the protective wall I had placed around it.

I started to focus on those angry memories during that period of the meditation. I didn't feel that I was in conflict with my mom, since we had had many moments of reconciliation and sincere apologies over the years. Still, during week 5, I chose her as the person I was in conflict with.

Immediately when I got to that point in the meditation and began to direct the words "May you feel joy without pain" to her, the tears started flowing, and I could barely breathe. I felt myself trying to shut off, and I heard her voice telling me to be a brave little soldier and not cry. Instead, I let myself be with the awareness of the feelings that were coming up for me. I realized in that moment, although there had been a reconciliation, a deep hurt had not been forgiven, and I needed to continue to focus my attention there to truly let go.

The Interconnectedness of the World Around Us

As I would say the phrase "May all beings feel protected and peaceful," my mind always created a very specific image, an expanding bubble of protection that would appear to cover and protect everyone and everything within it. It was like seeing a camera lens pulling out wider and wider to show the world around me and witness this protective bubble expanding.

It would begin with a picture of the small part of the world I occupied and the people I interacted with daily. I'd imagine the busyness of my Brooklyn street with restaurants and bars filled with people and the little park with dogs chasing each other. Then I'd pan out and see the entirety of the city and recognize all the buildings filled with people, the birds flying above Central Park. Then even farther out, seeing my entire state, then country, recognizing the vastness of the land and the millions of people and creatures each in need of loving-kindness. Then my vision would pull all the way out and recognize the billions of souls throughout the world all desiring loving-kindness. From my meditation cushion in

Brooklyn, I was a part of sending that loving-kindness out into the world.

After all these weeks of consistent practice, I found that this extension of loving-kindness to the world around me made me feel a sense of connection. As someone who had long searched for the connection of home, I finally was starting to feel that within me.

Passing It Forward

When I started the mindfulness instructor certification program through MNDFL, I aimed to go through the process to deepen my own understanding of mindfulness. However, through the masterful guidance of a team of amazing teachers including the Reverend angel Kyodo williams, David Perrin, Caverly Morgan, Jackie Stewart, and more, I found a deep appreciation for the art of teaching mindfulness. After fulfilling all requirements for certification, I started teaching meditation classes at a studio in New York City. The first class I was scheduled to teach was Loving-Kindness Meditation. Remembering my first experience of that meditation, I wanted to make sure that any first-timers understood that they might not have an immediate transcendent experience, and that was perfectly all right. I asked new students to raise their hands. Claire reported that she had never participated in Loving-Kindness Meditation before. I told her to be patient and that I'd love to hear about her experience after the class.

I led the class through the meditation and had a group discussion about their experience afterward. Many of the students were moved and had questions about what emotional experiences were coming up for them and shared how connected they felt to a sense of loving-kindness, but Claire was particularly quiet. As everyone was leaving, I asked how her experience was. I could tell that she had wanted to sneak off without saying anything, but she just said it was good but she found it really hard to keep her mind focused. I told her the story of my first class and what a terrible experience it had been and how I had vowed never to do a Loving-Kindness Meditation again. I also explained how, over time, it had become an integral part of my practice and was a major reason why I had pursued my certification. I could tell that Claire felt relieved to hear that it was normal not to have a magical first experience with loving-kindness. In fact, she shared about how, had I not spoken to her, she would have not returned. I challenged her to take seven weeks and make it a consistent daily practice and see what might shift for her.

For the next few weeks, Claire attended class with me each Tuesday and gave me an update on how her daily practice was going. She was open and honest about her experience, and it was lovely to see her go through many of the stages of growth that I had gone through. She had experiences of boredom, anger, frustration, and moments where she could feel her heart softening and opening up to the world around her. After several weeks, she let me know that one of the relationships she felt had transformed the most was with her ex-boyfriend, who had shattered her heart and she never felt she could forgive. Seeing him as a human instead of a monster was challenging. She struggled to hold on to the anger instead of releasing it, but as the weeks went by, she slowly was getting to a place where the hold his action had on her didn't feel as intense. And while she had no intention of letting him back in her life, for her own well-being, she felt comfortable working toward a place of forgiveness.

The Process of Leading with Love

Incorporating loving-kindness into a daily practice can be transformative for leading with love and compassion in your life. Here's a step-by-step process to help you integrate loving-kindness into your daily routine and begin to lead with love.

Step 1: Set Aside Time Each Day

Choose a specific time each day to dedicate to your Loving-Kindness Meditation. This could be in the morning upon waking, during a break in your day, or before bedtime. Consistency is key, so try to stick to your chosen time every day. (Challenge yourself to do this for seven weeks for 5 to 30 minutes a day.)

Step 2: Find a Quiet Space

Find a quiet and comfortable space where you can sit undisturbed for a few minutes. It could be a corner of your home, a peaceful outdoor spot, or anywhere else you feel relaxed and at ease.

Step 3: Set Your Intention

Begin your practice by setting a clear intention to cultivate loving-kindness and compassion for yourself and others. You might say a simple phrase like "May I lead with love and compassion in all that I do."

Step 4: Focus on Your Breath

Close your eyes and take a few deep breaths to center yourself and bring your awareness to the present moment. Notice the sensation of your breath as it enters and leaves your body, using it as an anchor for your practice.

Step 5: Cultivate Loving-Kindness

Start by directing loving-kindness toward yourself, then a dear one, then a neutral person, then someone with whom you've had conflict, then the world around you. Silently repeat loving-kindness phrases, such as

- May (I, you, or all beings) be happy.
- May (I, you, or all beings) be healthy.
- May (I, you, or all beings) be safe.
- May (I, you, or all beings) live with ease.

Step 6: Reflect on Your Experience

Take a few moments to reflect on your practice and notice how it feels in your body and mind. Notice any shifts in your mood or perspective, and observe any feelings of warmth, compassion, or connection that arise.

Step 7: Integrate Loving-Kindness into Your Day

Carry the feelings of loving-kindness and compassion with you as you go about your day. Use them as a guiding principle in your interactions and decision making, leading with love and empathy in all that you do.

Calm Kit Tool #10: Loving-Kindness (Metta) Meditation

Loving-Kindness (Metta) Meditation is rooted in the Buddhist tradition and involves cultivating feelings of love, compassion, and goodwill toward oneself and others. The practice typically involves repeating phrases or mantras of loving-kindness directed toward oneself, loved ones, acquaintances, difficult individuals, and eventually all beings everywhere. Here are the steps for practicing Loving-Kindness (Metta) Meditation. (A full script for the meditation can be found in Chapter 14.)

1. **Prepare for meditation.** Find a quiet and comfortable space where you can sit or lie down without distractions. Close your eyes if it feels comfortable, or maintain a soft gaze.
2. **Set your intention.** Begin by setting a clear intention for your practice. You might choose cultivating love, compassion, or inner peace.
3. **Cultivate loving-kindness toward yourself.** Start by directing loving-kindness toward yourself. Repeat silently or aloud phrases of loving-kindness, such as
   - May I be happy.
   - May I be healthy.
   - May I be safe.
   - May I live with ease.
4. **Extend loving-kindness to others.** Once you've cultivated loving-kindness toward yourself, gradually extend it to others. Start with someone you love unconditionally, such as a close friend or family member, then a neutral person, and then someone with whom you've had conflict. Repeat the same phrases of loving-kindness for them:
   - May you be happy.
   - May you be healthy.
   - May you be safe.
   - May you live with ease.

5. **Extend loving-kindness to all beings.** Finally, broaden your practice to include all beings everywhere. Repeat the phrases of loving-kindness for all beings, wishing them happiness, health, safety, and ease:
   - May all beings be happy.
   - May all beings be healthy.
   - May all beings be safe.
   - May all beings live with ease.
6. **Cultivate feelings of loving-kindness.** As you repeat the phrases of loving-kindness, allow yourself to truly feel the sentiments behind the words. Visualize sending waves of love, compassion, and goodwill to yourself and others, cultivating a deep sense of warmth and connection.
7. **Stay present and open.** Throughout the practice, stay present with your experience and remain open to whatever arises. If you encounter resistance or difficulty, offer yourself compassion and continue with the practice.
8. **Conclude the practice.** When you feel ready, gently bring your practice to a close. Take a few deep breaths, allowing yourself to bask in the feelings of love, compassion, and connection you've cultivated. Carry these feelings with you as you go about your day, allowing them to infuse your interactions and experiences with greater kindness and understanding.

By practicing Loving-Kindness (Metta) Meditation, you can cultivate a deep sense of calm, compassion, and connection in your life, toward both yourself and others.

13 Finding Forgiveness

A Gentle Reminder

There's a freedom that comes from being able to release the burden of someone else's actions. Anyone who has been hurt and wronged in life knows it's never easy to move forward and lean into forgiveness, but if the weight you're carrying is so heavy that it's impacting how you walk through life, it may be time to consider what unburdening yourself would feel like. Forgiveness is not necessarily for the other person but rather for yourself. It's handing back what has been on your shoulders for far too long and letting the person who has wronged you know you are at peace with the fact that the burden of their actions is no longer yours to hold. It's a process of uncovering your worth and recognizing what you deserve. There's never an obligation to forgive, but if holding on is costing more than letting go, it may be time to start the process of letting go.

Abrightness and kindness about Daniel shone through despite his shy demeanor. He was careful with his words and chose to share himself with me in small bits, slowly opening up as the weeks passed but always keeping things close to his chest. Whereas most people share their story during our first session with so much detail that by the time they finish, we're nearly out of time, Daniel merely gave me a short list of facts about himself, almost as if we were at an ice breaker at a new hire orientation. It was clear that trust needed to be established before Daniel would truly open up, and it was my job to establish a space of safety while that trust could be built.

During our first session, Daniel mentioned that he had been facing a great deal of anxiety and had suffered several panic attacks over the past few months. He also was not sleeping and was having terrible nightmares when he did manage to fall asleep. And most concerning to him was the constant voice of his inner gremlin (Chapter 5) that was berating him, making him feel a constant sense of guilt and shame and blame. He had found me through my online meditation videos and gained some relief through them. He wanted to get a better understanding of the work I did and how and why the short relaxation videos seemed to be working for him.

Over the next few months, Daniel told me his story in more depth. He shared what life was like growing up in a small border town in southern Texas and the honor and pride his family felt for their heritage, having moved to the United States a generation earlier. He spoke of his parents' efforts to teach their children English so they could thrive in their new country while still ensuring that they remembered and honored their native tongue at home. And he mentioned the sadness he felt when he was on the phone with his mom and forgot a word in Spanish due to lack of daily practice. Daniel was the first and only member of his family to graduate high school. Thanks to a supportive high school teacher who recognized his talents and capacity for learning, he applied to college. The day his acceptance letter came from Stanford was a pivotal moment in his life and changed everything. He had to explain to his family what this honor meant and admit to his father that he would not be following the traditional role expected of a man in his family. With no one in his family to look to for guidance, Daniel made the decision to leave on his own. The good-bye with his mother was emotional; his father chose not to be there. Daniel boarded the bus and headed out without as much as a hug.

His time at Stanford was both wonderful and terrifying as he left his small town for the first time and tried to adapt to his new life, surrounded by people unlike him. But in some ways he felt a sense of relief in being away from home. While he had great respect and love for his family, his upbringing had been far from easy. He was always seen as different and was bullied at school, targeted for being too studious or the teacher's pet or not masculine enough, as he was never interested in sports or girls. This bullying often continued at home when his father returned from work.

Although Daniel continued to thrive in school despite the abuse, the message that he was inherently flawed grew within him, and no amount of success or distance was going to change that at the time. And Daniel had a great deal of success at Stanford as both an academic and an athlete. While he was not interested in contact sports, running was a way for him to soothe himself and be in motion even though he mostly felt stuck.

After he graduated with a degree in economics, he received a prestigious job offer in New York, taking him across the country and even farther away from his family. His parents' reaction to the job offer was mixed; after a lot of soul searching, Daniel decided to follow the opportunity. When we met, he had spent the last ten years away, returning home only a handful of times. He exceled at work but constantly felt like he was fighting demons. Each day he showed up fully at work, where he appeared to glide through his workday with grace and ease. Underneath that calm exterior he was working hard to keep himself together. He was like the duck that looks so smooth and graceful gliding through the water; no one sees the legs beneath the surface treading furiously to keep the duck afloat.

Over time I learned many of the details of Daniel's story, but I sensed he was still holding some parts close. I knew that to help him find the sense of self-love and belonging that he was looking for, he'd need to confront some of those darker parts, so during one session I asked if he would be willing to start to explore the gremlin voice and that feeling of guilt and shame. He agreed.

Uncovering the Dragon

During that session, we went through Gremlin Discovery Technique, as discussed in Chapter 5, and identified the messages that his inner gremlin voice was sending. We also began to create an image of the personification of that voice and what it would sound like. For Daniel, this gremlin voice was a dragon named Draco who scorched the earth around him and cautioned him to never share the intimate parts of himself with anyone. Draco reminded Daniel that who he was

was not acceptable and that it wasn't safe to let people see the real him. To keep him from experiencing the shame and embarrassment he felt as a child when people noticed who was, Draco reminded him of all the things that were wrong with him, pointing out every flaw, both physical and internal.

When Daniel started drawing awareness to that part of himself and removing the attachment to that voice being true, he began to see how deeply the negative thoughts had impacted him. Now he could see how he had internalized what the kids at school had teased him about and what his father reminded him of. In discovering this, he realized how deeply by these messages had impacted him and how his distance and separation from his family made sense. He was just realizing that the distance he created from home was not only for job prospects and a better life; it kept him from having to deal with his father, a man he loved but was unable to forgive.

Daniel didn't share with me the specifics of what needed to be forgiven, and I never pushed, but I did ask if he would be interested in a homework assignment of sorts: to write the full story of what happened in those moments with his father that led him here, painting the full picture and telling his story. I told him there was no expectation for him to share the story with anyone, but when he felt comfortable, he could share as much or as little as he liked in our sessions, with the therapist he was also seeing, or with someone close to him. The important thing was to let his story be heard when the time was right.

Telling the Story

There is so much value in being able to put voice to your story and share it with a trusted source. When we've been hurt by someone, we tend to keep the whole story to ourselves and take on the burden. This is especially true with those we love the most who have hurt us. Our love for them can keep us from sharing their actions with anyone, because we fear that in telling our story, we will hurt them in some way. We would rather take on the pain than risk hurting them, even when they have hurt us deeply. But it's important for everyone to remember that our stories are ours to share. Holding stories in causes harm to no one but ourselves.

Daniel went home and worked through the homework. He wrote down his story in great detail and felt inspired to email what he had written to me prior to our next session. As I read through Daniel's brave and vulnerable story, I gained a much clearer picture of who he was and what he had been through. When he came to our next session, he asked if he could read the story aloud to me. Quietly and with fear, he told me about a lifetime of not feeling good enough, of being bullied, criticized for every aspect of who he was, and made to feel like he was broken and bad. His father's temper raged; he came home from work each night and took his anger out on the family. To protect his mother and sisters, Daniel voluntarily took the abuse, sitting close-lipped and tight-fisted as his father hurled a barrage of vitriol at him. The anger was much like the anger Draco from the Gremlin Discovery Technique showed Daniel each night. But in the aftermath of those nights of abuse from his father at home, Daniel still felt love and duty to be the son he was supposed to be. So he attempted to change himself, to hide or remove the things his father critiqued him for, and to be the perfect version of the son he felt he needed to be to stop the rage. But it never worked and the rage continued, both from his father and internally, even after he had left the home. He went on to describe his life being one of constantly needing to prove and to hide parts of himself to protect himself from the pain his father had caused. This need for protection required Daniel to separate from his family. He felt a longing to go home, but he recognized that to do so, he would need to reconcile things and forgive the man who had caused this pain. Despite his efforts, Daniel wasn't ready to forgive.

Getting Angry

Although the initial sharing of the story felt empowering for Daniel and as if a weight had been lifted, during our next session, he was quiet and removed. He was concerned with what the story had brought up for him. All of those feelings had been dormant for so long; now that had they had spilled out on the page, they were so present in his life. There was sadness, fear, hurt, but most uncomfortable for him was this anger. The kind of anger that he fought so hard against in his life, the anger that he wouldn't reveal at work, the anger that he remembered coming from his dad on those scary nights at home. And it was causing him to feel a lack of control.

In that moment, we started to normalize his anger, to highlight that it made sense, given everything he had gone through growing up. He was justified in that anger. That it was OK to feel anger, and it was OK to express that anger. We just needed to figure out how he wanted to express it. I guided him through the Anger RAID Meditation (Chapter 11), which allowed for him to slowly begin to recognize his anger, allow it to be present, investigate how it was showing up for him, and determine what he wanted to do in the face of that anger.

Daniel began to allow the anger to be present, to investigate those feelings beneath it—the hurt, the betrayal, the pain, the sadness. And then he began to tap into the initial impulse to action in the face of this anger: to scream, to let it out, to cuss and say all the things he'd been holding in for years. In the calm space of our session, he gave himself permission to let it all out. And I held space for him as he did so. When the anger began to subside, the tears of release came. I held space for those as well, not needing to fix things or make things better. And after the storm of emotions came a calm and clarity Daniel hadn't felt for years. We ended the session with a homework assignment of finding ways to express anger throughout the week, to pause in the face of it and reflect on how he can express that anger rather than internalize it.

It was an uncomfortable week for him, but Daniel continued to show up for himself in moments of anger. He found that allowing people to know when he was upset was not only liberating but actually got things done. He found that, unlike his father, he could control that anger and use it to express himself without needing to yell. And as he continued to sit with anger when it came up, the concept of returning home and working toward forgiveness started to stir within him. He wasn't ready just yet, but he wrote to let me know that he wanted to explore it in our next session, so we did just that over the next few weeks.

Calculating the Costs

When working with clients, I like to tap into their worldview, to understand how they make decisions, what their superpowers and passions are, and what they avoid. From there, I try to create learning opportunities that make sense to them. Daniel's background in economics and his business prowess made him an analytical thinker who could examine every detail of a problem, understand the risks and uncertainties, make careful considerations given the benefits and potential costs, and confidently make decisions and adjust if necessary.

As he started to look at potentially forgiving his father, I asked whether we could remove his emotional connection to the decision and view it as we would a financial situation at work. I asked Daniel what it would look like to put the possibility of forgiveness through a financial model that would enable him to make a sound decision based on fact and logic.

The following week, he walked me through a thorough, detailed decision-making model that outlined the first step in this process: calculating the cost of *not* forgiving his father. His job was to look at every angle and begin quantifying the emotional burdens and calculating the financial costs he was incurring by not forgiving. He detailed the impact that it had on his career, the stress it caused on his relationships, and the ability to show up as a son and be part of his family's heritage. He noted the financial cost of years of therapy and coaching, and he even went as far as to include the cost of wine for those nights when it all felt too much. When he sketched it all out, he was able to look at the cost of the burden he'd held for so long and how it was impacting his future.

One of the things we discussed was the concept of sunk costs and how, in business, he would never make a decision based on past costs and investments. He gave me the example of buying an expensive concert ticket and getting really sick hours before the event and trying to decide whether to go, knowing that going would be dangerous and you'd risk getting sicker. Because you'd already paid for the ticket, the money you spent is considered a sunk cost. You can't get a refund, so whether you attend the concert or not, the cost is already incurred and cannot be recovered. It's important not to make the decision based solely on the cost of the ticket but rather on what's best for your well-being in the moment.

In many ways, Daniel realized that he was allowing the cost of the past to determine the course of his future—something he would never do in his business life.

Determining the Value

With the recognition of what holding on to the anger toward his father was costing him, I asked Daniel to map out the value of letting go of the burden that he'd been carrying for so long. What would he gain by forgiving his father? Over the next week, he worked his magic with numbers and came back with another detailed spreadsheet that highlighted what was possible for him.

Through his analysis, he could see that letting go of the burden of resentment toward his father would open up a multitude of possibilities in his life. He could cultivate healthier relationships, both with his family members and with himself, free from the constraints of past grievances. With forgiveness, he saw the potential to experience greater emotional well-being and reduced stress and gain a sense of inner peace. He envisioned reclaiming his personal power and autonomy, no longer allowing past hurts to dictate his present and future. When he looked at everything, he recognized that forgiveness would pave the way for authentic connection, deeper intimacy, and a renewed sense of purpose and fulfillment in his life.

From there Daniel was able to make a sound decision based on facts and logic. He was ready to begin the process of letting go and lean into forgiveness. The decision was made, but the hard part had just begun.

Finding Empathy

In our sessions, we often talked about Daniel's ability to empathize with others in such a profound way, how he was able to understand others at work. Even when they behaved in a way that made his job harder, he could approach them with compassion and care. But Daniel couldn't understand why his father had treated him the way he had. Daniel tried to put himself in his father's shoes and imagine having a son like him, but he knew there was no way that he could treat a child like that, especially since Daniel had excelled in school, never got in trouble, helped out at home, and did all the right things. His father's attitude made no logical sense to him, so he couldn't see a way to empathize with him. To Daniel, his father was a monster.

During one of our sessions, I led Daniel through an exercise to explore a sense of radical empathy. The intention was not for Daniel to reach a point where he could acknowledge that his father's behavior was acceptable or to excuse the man's behavior in any way, but for him to examine the situation from his father's worldview. Perhaps empathy and understanding were possible with a different perspective. It's reasonable to assume that when we are wronged or hurt by a person, their actions come as a result of who *we* are; through radical empathy, sometimes we can uncover a deeper reason for the behavior and see that we were simply in their line of fire. In that situation, anyone would have been treated the same way; we just happened to be an innocent bystander.

Over the hour, we removed emotion and connection and began to explore the Empathetic Inquiry process (Chapter 10). Although many things about their relationship needed to be addressed, right now we explored why his father couldn't accept who Daniel was and why his father chose to spend his life making Daniel feel small and worthless. This had always stuck with him as such a cruel and awful thing to do to your child, and he couldn't understand why his father would do that.

As we walked through each of the questions, Daniel began to develop a deeper understanding of who his father was. He began to explore the situation with a sense of radical empathy for the older man. Given everything Daniel uncovered during this exercise, he started to see that his father was protecting himself from his own fears more than purposefully hurting Daniel. Beneath all the older man's actions was a deep hurt and a deep fear that had little to do with who his son was.

His father's actions were hurtful and Daniel could not justify them, but he could empathize with what his father was going through that led to his inability to accept a son who was so different from him and so far removed from the traditional ideas of manhood he had been raised with. And with that empathy he was able to see that most likely his father was feeling a lot of pain, which he had no outlet for. That shift in perspective allowed Daniel to stop blaming himself for his father's actions and see the situation in a new light.

Recognizing Your Worth

Over the next few weeks, we worked on recognizing what Daniel had lost by not having a relationship with his father. The one thing that stood out the most was his sense of worth;

years of internalizing his father's words prevented Daniel from viewing himself as worthy. He saw himself as broken and constantly felt the need to prove himself to be seen as merely good. Developing a sense of self-love and worth is never an easy process, and this was the focus of the bulk of our sessions for a while before Daniel was able to see himself as someone who was whole, worthy, and far from broken.

We used several exercises and tools to get him to that point, but the Loving-Kindness (Metta) Meditation (Chapter 12) was pivotal in both his acceptance of himself and his ability to prepare to move forward with reconciliation with his father. I asked Daniel to come up with a set of phrases that would remind him that he was whole and loved, phrases he would send to himself as well as to loved ones, including his father. The phrases he chose were:

- May you be filled with loving-kindness.
- May you be held with a loving heart.
- May you see your inherent goodness and trust that you are loved.
- May you know your worth.

The practice of loving-kindness became a daily habit for Daniel, and over time it allowed for him to deepen his capacity for love and strengthen the relationships in his life, especially with himself. Eventually he felt that his inner gremlin voice was less intense and more distant. For the first time he connected with what it felt like to experience a loving relationship with himself. This practice also allowed Daniel to connect with that sense of empathy he had developed for his father. With the grounded feeling that came from recognizing his worth and cultivating a sense of self-love, he was able to start to look forward toward a future worth living instead of feeling stuck.

Releasing the Vision

The next area we focused on was the loss of the future he had hoped for with his father. He had always believed that if he worked hard enough, was good enough, and proved himself, he would be able to have a father who saw him as special, one who called him to let him know he was loved, one who bragged about him to his friends and loved him unconditionally.

Part of letting go was to release the vision that he had created, mourn the loss of a desired relationship with his father, and accept him for who he was capable of being in his life. In many ways this was like a death in itself, but in letting go Daniel was able to see how striving to create that world was having an impact on so many areas of his life and keeping him stuck in this pattern of striving for perfection and dealing with inevitable disappointment. Together we went through the process of letting go (Chapter 7). When Daniel was able to let go of the future he was trying to force into being, he was able to start to see a future worth walking toward.

Creating a New Vision

Daniel started to craft a vision for his life, one that wasn't contingent on his father being anything but what he could be and one that removed the need for parental approval in order to feel worthy.

During this process of crafting his vision, we worked through an exercise of removing the traditional thoughts of future. We didn't focus on what his career progression would entail or what his house or car would look like. Instead, we zoned in who he wanted to be in the world. He wanted to connect with the emotions he wanted more of: joy, hope, and serenity. He wanted to uphold in his life certain core values: authenticity, kindness, love. What areas of his life needed to shift? He needed to own his worth, to trust himself, to show up in his life not to prove himself but to connect with others and share himself fully. And finally, we asked: What did he want most for himself? The answer here was clear: He wanted to be free.

The statement Daniel created for himself was this: "I'm building a life filled with joy, hope, and serenity, one where I lead with authenticity, kindness, and love, while the past no longer defines me and I am able to own my worth, trust myself, and show up for life not to prove myself but to share myself, so that ultimately I'm free."

And with that vision in place and serving as a guide for his life, I asked one final question: What was he willing to let go of in order to get there? Daniel started to hear a host of things from his life, but the most pressing was that he needed to stop allowing the past with his father to impact him. And his decision in that moment was to forgive his father so that he could move forward and stop holding on to anger any longer.

Freedom Found

In our last session, Daniel told me that he had flown home to be with his family the prior weekend, and he was able to sit down and speak with his father. He was able to approach the conversation with both openness and honesty, letting his father know the work he had done around their past and how he felt he could understand much of what happened, but there was still so much that he needed to know. He opened up with empathy and understanding and told his father that he truly wanted him to be part of his life again and hoped that they could both forgive each other and start the path forward.

It was the start of something new, and both men were able to begin the process of reconciliation. Daniel mentioned it felt like a huge weight had been lifted from his shoulders. Because of the work he had done around forgiveness, Daniel now clearly saw that the cost of holding on to anger and internalizing the pain inflicted on him by his father was too much. Throughout the process of forgiving, Daniel also learned to value himself and see that he was worthy of more than he was allowing himself to be. But most important, he learned that it wouldn't have mattered how his father reacted or whether he received an apology from his father, because the value of forgiveness wasn't tied to his father anymore; it was tied to Daniel's own freedom.

The Process of Finding Forgiveness

The process of finding forgiveness is described next.

Step 1: Tell Your Story

Begin by acknowledging the weight of the emotions you carry. Holding on to your story can cause harm only to yourself. Consider starting a writing project or sharing your feelings with a trusted friend or therapist. By giving voice to your experiences, you begin the process of healing.

Step 2: Get Angry

Recognize and honor your right to feel angry about what has been done to you. Allow yourself to fully experience this emotion. Revisit techniques such as the Anger RAID Meditation (Chapter 11) to help navigate and process your anger in a healthy way.

Step 3: Calculate the Cost

Take stock of the toll that holding on to this anger is exacting on your life. Assess whether you are allowing past hurts to dictate your future. Understanding the costs involved can motivate you to seek resolution and healing.

Step 4: Determine the Value

Reflect on what you stand to gain by embracing forgiveness. Consider the possibilities for personal growth and liberation that come with releasing resentment. Visualize a future free from the burden of anger, and envision the positive impact such a future could have on your life.

Step 5: Create a Space of Empathy and Understanding

Shift your perspective to consider the circumstances and experiences that may have led the other person to hurt you. Cultivate empathy by acknowledging their struggles and fears. Recognize that their actions may have been driven by their own pain rather than reflecting your worth.

Step 6: Recognize Your Worth

Begin to acknowledge the toll that holding on to anger has taken on you. Recognize your inherent value and worthiness. Embrace the belief that you deserve healing, peace, and happiness.

Step 7: Release the Vision of What Could Have Been

Acknowledge the loss associated with holding on to resentment. Allow yourself to mourn what could have been and let go of unrealistic expectations. By releasing attachment to past outcomes, you open yourself to new possibilities for growth and fulfillment.

Step 8: Envision a Future

Shift your focus toward envisioning the life you desire to live beyond your current circumstances. Visualize a future filled with joy, fulfillment, and purpose. Let this vision guide your journey toward healing and transformation.

Calm Kit Tool: Forgiveness Meditation

Forgiveness Meditation is a transformative exercise designed to release resentment, cultivate compassion, and foster healing within the self and toward others. Through guided reflection and deep introspection, this meditation empowers us to let go of past grievances, embrace forgiveness, and move forward with a sense of peace and liberation. Join this journey of self-discovery and compassion as we explore the profound power of forgiveness. The following steps are part of the Forgiveness Meditation. (A full script of the meditation is available in Chapter 14.)

1. **Reflect on self-forgiveness.** Think about times when you have caused harm to yourself, either intentionally or unintentionally. Acknowledge the pain you have caused yourself, and recognize that holding on to this resentment is harmful. Place your hand on your chest as a gesture of self-compassion and say words of forgiveness to yourself. Allow yourself to let go of any guilt or shame you may be carrying.

2. **Extend forgiveness to others.** Shift your focus to people who have caused you pain or harm. Visualize their faces and acknowledge the hurt they have caused you. Recognize that holding on to resentment toward them only perpetuates your own suffering. Offer words of forgiveness to them, releasing any anger or bitterness you may be holding on to.

3. **Seek forgiveness for your actions.** Reflect on times when you have caused harm to others through your words or actions. Acknowledge the pain you have caused them, and express genuine remorse. Ask for their forgiveness, and commit to making amends for your past actions.

4. **Release resentment and embrace forgiveness.** Take a few moments to breathe deeply and let go of any lingering feelings of resentment or anger. Embrace a sense of forgiveness and compassion toward yourself

and others. Allow yourself to experience a sense of peace and freedom as you release the weight of past grievances.

By acknowledging past grievances, extending forgiveness to ourselves and others, and embracing peace, we can move forward with a sense of liberation and compassion. Through regular practice, we can integrate forgiveness into our daily lives, nurturing self-compassion and fostering healthier relationships with others.

14 Meditations and Daily Habits for Honoring Connection

This final chapter is dedicated to nurturing and enhancing your connections with others through meditative practices and daily habits. We'll explore techniques designed to enrich your relationships, fostering empathy, understanding, loving-kindness, and forgiveness. These tools will help to deepen your ability to be present in relationships and to cultivate a profound sense of connection with the world around you.

Meditations for Connection

The following three meditations serve as powerful tools for honoring and repairing connections with others. The Anger RAID Meditation involves acknowledging and exploring feelings of anger in a safe and controlled manner, allowing you to understand the root causes of your anger and cultivate compassion toward yourself and others. By navigating anger with mindfulness and empathy, you can foster healthier responses and prevent conflicts from escalating, thus preserving relationships. The Loving-Kindness (Metta) Meditation cultivates feelings of compassion, empathy, and goodwill toward yourself and others, promoting a sense of interconnectedness and strengthening bonds. Through this practice, you develop a deep appreciation for the humanity of others, fostering understanding and empathy even in times of conflict or disagreement. The Forgiveness Meditation guides you through the process of letting go of resentment and grudges, offering forgiveness to yourself and others. By releasing the emotional burden of past grievances, you can heal wounds, restore trust, and rebuild connections with others, ultimately fostering greater harmony and reconciliation in relationships. Together, these meditative practices provide transformative pathways for honoring, repairing, and nurturing connections with others, fostering empathy, understanding, and reconciliation.

Anger RAID Meditation

RAID stands for *recognize, allow, investigate,* and *determine next steps.* The Anger RAID Meditation provides a structured framework for acknowledging and processing anger in a constructive way. By recognizing, allowing, investigating, and determining next steps, you can cultivate greater self-awareness and emotional intelligence. This meditation encourages you to approach anger with curiosity and compassion, empowering you to respond to challenging emotions with wisdom and skill. Through this meditation, you can honor the presence of anger while finding constructive ways to address its underlying causes and transform it into positive action. This meditation is based on Tara Brach's RAIN meditation; rather than sitting in a place of nurturing of intense emotions, as the *n* in Brach's RAIN meditation encourages, you begin to determine and take action to move you forward.

Begin by finding a safe space to find comfort and stillness. Allow your body to connect with what's beneath you. Feel a sense of rooting as you allow your body to sink into the seat or the chair and let your hands fall gently on your lap.

Start by either closing your eyes or keeping a gentle, soft focus with your eyes gazing downward and begin to allow yourself to connect to the breath, breathing in and breathing out. As you breathe, allow your body to soften and allow yourself to connect to the anger that is present for you today. Begin to scan through your body and note the spaces of the body that are holding on to that anger. Some typical spaces might be a tightness in the shoulders, the heart beating quickly, the stomach feeling tense or tight . . . wherever that anger is being held, just allow or it to be there, removing judgment or the need for it to go away. Let it be present for you in this moment right here, right now. Take a few moments to sit with the anger, feeling the physical connection, the emotional connection, allowing it to be present for you.

Now begin to turn your attention to the heart, connecting to that emotional pull and feeling into the anger that's present. Allow the mind to connect with the thoughts of anger for the next few

(*continued*)

moments. There's no need to stop the thoughts; let them take you to where they need to. Allow those thoughts to be present, allow the physical sensations of anger to be present, and allow the emotion of anger to sit at the center. With a deep breath in and a deep breath out, allow those thoughts, the physical sensations, and the emotional connections to drop almost as if they could settle into the ground beneath you. Then connect back to the heart and begin to investigate what might be under the anger. So often anger blankets deeper feelings of sadness, shame, or embarrassment. Allow yourself to start to investigate those emotions that might be blanketed by the anger. As you allow those emotions to come to the forefront, start to investigate how they connect to the body, how those emotions connect to the mind. Without judgment, let it all be present: the anger, the sadness, the shame, the embarrassment, the fear. See if there's anything you can learn from this experience. Is there anything that this anger is trying to teach you or warn you about?

Now, with a deep breath in and a deep breath out, let all those emotions begin to drop and settle into the ground beneath you. From here, begin to note any impulses to action in the face of anger. Maybe it's to fight, maybe it's to run, maybe it's to attack, but allow yourself to begin to bring to mind the instinct to action that is present for you at this moment.

Then, from this centered space, connected to the breath, begin to tune in to who you desire to be in the world; the person you want to show up as, the person deeply connected to your values, connected to the things that are meaningful and important to you. From that space of connection to that higher self, bring to mind the many options that might not come initially and determine how you would like to move forward through this anger connected to your higher self. Begin to determine what the best next step would be, the step that allows you to be aligned with your values and in integrity with who you want to be in the world.

With that sense of clarity, begin to return to your breath, return to your body, return to a sense of awareness of your surroundings. Experience the sounds, the smells, your senses of taste and touch. When it feels right and safe to do so, go ahead and flutter your eyes open, taking in the space around you and entering back connected and calm.

Loving-Kindness (Metta) Meditation

The Loving-Kindness, or Metta, Meditation provides a sense of relaxation and connection. Participants ground themselves in the present moment and visualize extending loving-kindness toward themselves, loved ones, neutrals, and those with whom they've had conflicts. This practice fosters empathy, understanding, and interconnectedness, promoting inner peace and enriching relationships. Research suggests that regular practice of Loving-Kindness Meditation can reduce stress, increase positive emotions, and enhance overall well-being. When they emerge from the meditation, participants often report feeling more connected, peaceful, and compassionate toward themselves and others, which highlights the profound benefits of cultivating loving-kindness in daily life.

Begin by closing your eyes or keeping a soft gaze downward and settling into the moment. Allow yourself to root down into what's beneath you, feeling your shoulders drop, feeling your belly get loose, not needing to hold on.

Start to draw awareness to your breath, the simple inhale and exhale, breathing in and breathing out.

And as you allow yourself to truly settle into the moment, start to allow your mind to settle. Just drop any thoughts that might be present. Start to draw your awareness to your imagination. Imagine a room full of people, and see yourself seated in a chair just looking around and seeing the many people surrounding you. Around you are the people you have known and loved throughout your life, but also within this room notice there are strangers, people you might have known vaguely in your past, people who look very different from you, people you might have had conflict with as well. No matter whom you look at, you begin to see a sense of love coming from everyone.

And as you stand up and begin to walk throughout the room, start to take in everyone's eyes, noting as you look into their eyes the feeling of love that comes through.

In the middle of all these people, stop to sense that feeling of love connected to you. And as you connect to that sense of loving-kindness within the room, start to direct these words to yourself, silently saying to yourself:

- May I be held in loving-kindness.
- May I feel joy without pain.
- May I feel protected and peaceful.
- May I feel connected and calm.
- May I be well.

Take a moment to allow that feeling of loving-kindness to just be present today. Feel into the sensations of connecting to that sense of loving-kindness directed toward you. And if any thoughts or feelings beyond those associated with loving-kindness start to arise, distracting you, allow them to be present and then to pass, continuing always to draw your attention back to loving-kindness.

Now scan the room once more, and look for a face that is familiar, a face that feels safe and warm, a face of a dear loved one. As you draw yourself closer and closer to them, stop and reach out to hold their hands, look into their eyes, and silently say:

- May you be held in loving-kindness.
- May you feel joy without pain.
- May you feel protected and peaceful.

(continued)

- May you feel connected and calm.
- May you be well.

Give yourself permission to feel into this exchange of loving-kindness with this dear one, noting what it feels like to give love and also to be in the presence of their love. Feel this exchange between the two of you, let it be present in this moment.

Now allow yourself to scan the room once more, and start to walk toward a face that is somewhat familiar but the person is neutral. Perhaps it's someone you've seen before; you might know their face but not their name. You've passed them on the street or seen them at the store. As you start to approach them, stop and look into their eyes. And with that same love and affection that you shared with the dear one, begin to extend these words to them silently:

- May you be held in loving-kindness.
- May you feel joy without pain.
- May you feel protected and peaceful.
- May you feel connected and calm.
- May you be well.

Take a moment to be in this exchange with this neutral person, feeling what it feels like to see them and to recognize their humanity and to extend those words to them.

Now look around the room once more and note, across the room, that person with whom you've been in conflict. As you see them, begin to feel how your body responds to them physically. Allow yourself to walk as close to them as you feel comfortable: close enough to see into their eyes, to recognize their humanity. If it feels safe and right to do so, go ahead and extend these words to them silently:

- May you be held in loving-kindness.
- May you feel joy without pain.
- May you feel protected and peaceful.
- May you feel connected and calm.
- May you be well.

Allow whatever needs to come up in this moment to be present. Give yourself a moment to just be in this exchange of loving-kindness with this person with whom you've been in conflict.

And then finally begin to notice all of the people in the room. As you begin to note all of these souls around you, realize that the entirety of the world exists right here, right now. And within that vision, begin to gather the people who are in your intimate circle, the people you know and interact with daily basis, and just allow them to be around you.

(*continued*)

Then allow yourself to gather an even larger group: all of the people who exist within your city or state. And as the circle gets larger and larger, you can feel its protective nature. As it gets larger and expands outward, moving into the entire world, all creatures, all beings surround you in this moment.

And as you start to connect with them, begin to feel in to that sense of love and kindness once more and silently say:

- May all beings be held in loving-kindness.
- May all beings feel joy without pain.
- May all beings feel protected and peaceful.
- May all beings feel connected and calm.
- May all beings be well.

Allow this feeling of loving-kindness that was extended to the entire world to come back to you. Note the exchange of love, kindness, care, and compassion with yourself, a loved one, a stranger, the person with whom you've had conflict, and the world around you, all these unique individuals connecting you to love.

Breathe that love in, taking a deep breath in and breathing out.

And when it feels right, go ahead and flutter your eyes open. Take in the space around you and enter back, feeling connected and calm. Bring that love, kindness, care, and compassion with you as you go forward into your day.

Forgiveness Meditation

The Forgiveness Meditation offers a transformative journey toward self-compassion and reconciliation. In a safe and serene environment, participants are guided through acknowledging self-inflicted pain, releasing grudges held against others, and seeking forgiveness for harm caused. Through gentle touch and affirmations, individuals embrace self-forgiveness, extend empathy toward those who have caused harm, and apologize for their own actions. This practice fosters healing, liberation, and a deeper sense of connection, empowering individuals to navigate life with compassion and understanding.

Begin to allow yourself to settle into a comfortable space, letting your body feel into a sense of relaxation, letting your mind settle and simply being here now.

Start by connecting to the breath, breathing in and breathing out, letting your shoulders soften, your belly be loose. Let yourself sink into what's beneath you. Close your eyes if it feels right and safe to do so, or maintain a gentle focus with your eyes gazing down.

In the stillness and silence of this meditation, begin to draw your mind to the events or circumstances in which you have caused yourself pain, the moments that you are unwilling or unable to forgive yourself for those times when, out of fear or anger or confusion, you have harmed yourself or others. Allow your hand to come onto your

(continued)

chest. If it feels right and safe to do so, begin to say these words:

> I acknowledge that things that I have done to harm myself knowingly and unknowingly. I recognize that my thoughts words or actions have caused harm. Although I may have acted out of pain, fear, or anger, I have held on to this for too long. Today I am ready to let go, to forgive, and to finally say the words "I forgive myself."

Take the next few moments to be in that space of forgiveness, truly letting go and extending empathy and compassion to yourself and releasing the burden of what you've been holding on to.

Next begin to draw your awareness to the events or circumstances in your life in which you have been harmed, those moments where someone caused you pain and you are still holding on, unable to forgive. Allow the people with whom you are carrying that grudge to become clear in your mind. See their faces, recognize their humanity, understand that they have their own pains and struggles. If it feels right and safe to do so, extend these words to them:

> I acknowledge the things you have done to harm me knowingly and unknowingly. Although you may have acted out of pain or fear or anger, I have held on to this for too long. Today I'm ready to let go, to forgive and to finally say the words "I forgive you."

Take the next few moments extending these words and these feelings to those who have harmed you, feeling the release and letting go.

Now draw your mind to the people in your life you may have harmed through your actions or inactions, the people you have caused pain in their lives. See their faces to remember the moments that caused that pain. If it feels right and safe to do so, extend these words to them:

I acknowledge the things I have done to harm you knowingly and unknowingly and recognize that my thoughts, words, or actions have caused you harm. Although I may have acted out of pain, fear, or anger, I have gone on too long letting you carry this burden. I ask for your forgiveness, knowing that it is not necessary but letting you know that I am sorry for the pain that I have caused.

Take the next few moments to continue to extend that feeling to the people whom you have harmed and to yourself for the harm you have caused. Allow yourself to connect with a sense of letting go, of acknowledging your part in all of the conflict. Recognize the freedom that comes from forgiveness.

Connect back to the room, connect back to your body and your breath in this moment. Begin to move anything that needs to be awakened. When it feels right and safe to do so, go ahead and flutter your eyes open, taking in the space around you, and enter back connected and calm.

Daily Habits for Connection

Integrating these daily habits into your daily routine will help to fortify your connections and nurture meaningful relationships. By incorporating these practices, you'll return to a space where you can begin to foster deeper bonds with others and enrich the quality of your interactions.

Daily Exploration of Empathy

Transforming empathy into a daily habit can greatly enrich our relationships and understanding of others. Dedicate a few minutes each day to a perspective-taking exercise. Choose someone you want to understand better: a friend, family member, coworker, or someone you've had disagreements with. Reflect on their experiences, thoughts, and emotions, imagining the challenges they face.

Put yourself in their shoes, envisioning life through their circumstances. Practice compassion and empathy toward their journey, even if it differs from your own. Journal your insights or quietly contemplate, allowing understanding to grow naturally. Commit to repeating this exercise regularly to deepen empathy and broaden your understanding of others' perspectives.

Daily Practice of Loving-Kindness

Cultivating loving-kindness can profoundly transform our relationships with ourselves and others, nurturing compassion, connection, and overall well-being. Create a daily habit of dedicating a few minutes to loving-kindness affirmations as bookends for the day, once in the morning and once before bed.

Settle into a quiet, comfortable space, allowing yourself to relax and breathe deeply. Silently or aloud, repeat affirmations like "May I be happy," "May I be healthy," "May I be safe," and "May I live with ease." Envision yourself surrounded by a circle of people sharing warmth and kindness. Extend these sentiments to loved ones, neutral people, those with whom you are in conflict, and eventually all beings. Let this start and end your day and be with you always.

Daily Practice of Letting Go

Establishing a daily habit of letting go involves dedicating time each day to reflect on past hurts and to release them. Find a quiet space where you can sit comfortably and without interruption. Close your eyes or soften your gaze, allowing yourself to settle into the present moment.

Begin by acknowledging any self-inflicted pain and releasing it with self-forgiveness. Then let go of grudges held against others by extending forgiveness to them. As you make this a regular practice, you'll find that it becomes easier to let go of resentment and anger, leading to increased emotional freedom and inner peace.

Over time, you'll notice a reduction in stress and anxiety as you cultivate a more compassionate and forgiving mindset. This daily habit not only benefits your mental and emotional well-being but also strengthens your relationships with yourself and others, fostering deeper connections and understanding.

Final Thoughts: Settled

During my coaching certification program, we were told that by learning to hold space for our clients and listen without judgment or bias, we would be providing opportunities for change not only within our clients' lives but also within our own. I recognized the same thing from my time teaching meditation and listening to my students process their emotions. It was through their openness and vulnerability that I was able to expand my awareness and understanding of mindfulness and continue to come home to myself and open myself to the world around me. Just as I learned the power of letting it settle from my preschool student Jack, I took away beautiful lessons from each of my clients and students and continue to pass any knowledge forward so we can all find a calmer space to land.

Lessons Learned

In this book, I took you through some of the lessons my clients taught me during my time with them as well as those learned through life experiences and from masterful teachers I've been lucky enough to study with. To end, I want to leave you with some of the greatest lessons I learned on my journey thus far.

Lessons Learned from Finding Calm

Here are the lessons to take away from Part 1, "Finding Calm."

Lesson 1: To Find a Space of Calm, We Need to First Find a Space of Presence

My time with Jack (Chapter 1) and my other students in that preschool classroom taught me many lessons, but the power of presence has always stayed with me. While mindfulness is by no means a magic cure-all for a dysregulated nervous system, the simplicity of drawing awareness to the present moment and recognizing our surroundings and senses can start to help us return to a space of calm and stillness. I consistently return to mindfulness-based activities, such as the 5-4-3-2-1 Calming Technique for Anxiety (Chapter 1), for myself and with clients to find a space of calm.

Lesson 2: The Tools We Need to Find Calm Are Sharpened Through Consistency and Patience

Life tends to lead you to where you're can learn the lessons you need, but you also need to be willing to show up for yourself and learn the lessons. Had I not shown up to that meditation class years ago and been guided through the Body Scan by Yuval (Chapter 2), I wouldn't have gained the basic understandings of mindfulness and meditation that allowed me to find a sense of relief. I also wouldn't have learned the valuable lesson that consistency and patience are the necessary building blocks of a strong practice. Over the years I have continued to return to that lesson and hold it as a cornerstone of my practice.

Lesson 3: Fear Is Often an Indicator That We're Moving Closer to the Things That Matter

There are many moments in my life when fear held me back from accomplishing things that I wanted. In most of those situations I allowed that voice in my head to tell me that the fear was justified and I would fail if I tried, so I was better off to step back and not allow myself to feel the pain of losing it. Witnessing Caleb (Chapter 3) almost throw away his shot at a lifelong dream because of fear solidified my understanding that, in some cases, we actually can use fear as an indicator that we are approaching something deeply meaningful and important to us. By recognizing that and moving forward in the face of fear, with the proper tools and techniques to help keep us calm amid the storm, we can stop letting fear keep us from our dreams.

Lesson 4: Just as Happiness Is Not a Destination to Be Reached, Neither Is Calm

Throughout my life I tried and strove for an existence that was devoid of strong emotions. I believed that calm was a feeling to be held on to forever; if I worked hard enough and focused my attention on doing the right practices or obtaining the right knowledge, I would be able to avoid feeling anything but stillness. I have since come to recognize that finding calm is a process of understanding what calm feels like and using that as a place to return to when life takes you away from center. The meditations and daily habits that we explored throughout this book (Chapters 4, 9, 14) are there to help guide you home when you're feeling lost.

Lessons Learned from Coming Home to Yourself

Here are the lessons to take away from Part 2, "Coming Home to Yourself."

Lesson 5: We Are Not Our Thoughts, and When We Become Aware of Them, We Gain the Ability to Make Conscious Choices That Are in Our Best Interest

Our minds are constantly running with stories, images, memories, and opinions, and it's easy to identify with every thought that crosses our minds. Logic tends to tell us that if we have an angry thought, we must be angry. If we have a sad thought, we must be sad, and if we think that we're not smart enough, we are not smart enough. We hold on to these thoughts as truth because we never stop to observe them to decide if they are worth listening to or not. When I started to understand the concept of mindful awareness of thought and gained an understanding of my inner gremlin voice (Chapter 5), I learned just how empowering it can be to recognize our thoughts as separate from ourselves and to not be attached to them.

Lesson 6: Sometimes We Need a Reference Point to Return to in Order to Remind Us of What True Love Feels Like

Self-love was probably the most difficult concept for me to grasp. It took a lot for me to learn how to develop a sense of self-love and compassion for myself. My awakening came during a meditation class one day when Yuval led us through a Loving-Kindness Meditation centered on utilizing a loved one's care for us to feel a sense of love for ourselves. That moment helped give me a glimpse into the beauty of self-love and compassion and was only strengthened by my client Andrea (Chapter 6). The Self-Love Guided Visualization let me truly understand how powerful our minds can be and how connecting to the physical and emotional sensations we feel when we are loved can help us lean into those feelings and share them internally. That visualization has become a staple of my practice and has been seen and used by over 16 million people around the world through social media.

Lesson 7: To Move Forward, We Need to Let Go Not Only of the Past but Also of the Version of the Future We Envisioned

The feeling of longing for something that hasn't yet happened can be incredibly motivating and gives us a way to navigate through our present using that desired vision of the future as a guiding light. With most things in our lives, we begin to craft visions of our future connected to our present. We think about our current job and dream of the promotions we'll receive over the years and what we'll do with the raises. We think of staying connected to our childhood best friend and dream of raising our children down the street from each other. And as I discovered with Stephanie (Chapter 7), we dream of the future we'll build with our significant other and map out an entire lifetime of moments to be had. When circumstances beyond our control step in, we must mourn the loss of something that we never experienced, a future imagined but never lived. Stephanie's journey taught me the importance of creating a vision of a future that is aligned with your own desires and of letting go of old desires attached to what you're moving away from. This process has helped many of my clients move through some of their most difficult moments.

Lesson 8: When You Begin to Come Home to Yourself, It Doesn't Come All at Once, but Through a Series of Moments

Coming home to yourself is not a sudden event but rather a gradual journey that unfolds through a series of moments (Chapter 8). Each moment of self-awareness, self-acceptance, and self-compassion is like a stepping stone leading you closer to the essence of who you are. On my own journey, I learned the importance of recognizing that the process of self-discovery is ongoing and that growth occurs in increments, not in leaps and bounds. Just as a house is built brick by brick, coming home to yourself is a cumulative process, shaped by the accumulation of experiences, insights, and reflections. Cherish each moment along the way, for collectively they pave the path toward a deeper connection with yourself and guide you home.

Lessons Learned from Honoring Connection

Here are the lessons to take away from Part 3, "Honoring Connection."

Lesson 9: While Sympathy Is a Nod of Recognition from a Distance, Empathy Extends a Hand and Walks Alongside Another Through Their Joys and Sorrows

I always considered myself to be an empathetic person, but my work with Barbara (Chapter 10) helped me to understand empathy on a deeper level and see the power that can come when we're able to recognize another's worldview. The work we did together in separating sympathy from empathy helped me create the empathetic inquiry questions. I use these questions frequently to help clients understand their relationship with others and with themselves and to deepen their ability to extend empathy.

Lesson 10: There Are No Good or Bad Emotions, Simply Reactions to Our Circumstances That We Get to Decide to Let Guide Us or Not

From Ethan (Chapter 11), I learned to navigate through anger and that even our strongest emotions are not inherently bad. Anger is not something to be feared; rather it's a reaction to the world around us. At times those reactions are heightened due to past experiences, but when we draw awareness to our emotions without judgment, we begin to make conscious decisions on what is best for us and avoid being mindlessly controlled by our emotions. I often use the Anger RAID Meditation that I worked through with Ethan for myself and to help corporate clients begin to recognize, allow, investigate, and determine where to go in the face of anger.

Lesson 11: When We Begin to Lead with Loving-Kindness, We Open Ourselves to a Deeper Understanding of the Human Condition and See the Humanity That Exists in All of Us

The consistency and patience that I honed over the years was key to my understanding of the impact that loving-kindness (Chapter 12) can have on a life. Had I given up and let my initial impression of the meditation stand, I never would have been able to learn the important lessons that loving-kindness can teach us: that an interconnectedness exists between us all and that by opening ourselves up to give loving-kindness, we begin to see all beings, including ourselves, as worthy of love.

Lesson 12: There Is a Freedom to Be Found in Letting Go of the Constraints of the Past and Forging a New Vision for the Future

Finally, Daniel (Chapter 13) was integral in showing me the power of forgiveness. During the year that Daniel was working to find a space of forgiveness for his father, I was working to find a similar place with my mom. The feelings of anger and discomfort that were showing up in me during those early Loving-Kindness (Metta) Meditations made me take a deep look at my own journey of forgiveness via Forgiveness Meditation and see the resentment that I was holding on to in my life that needed to be addressed.

As I became more settled in my life and allowed emotions to have a place at the table, I realized I had never truly processed those words that my mom had said to me so many years ago. I had been marching forward as the brave little soldier she had told me to be, and I was unable to grieve the loss or feel the pain that I needed to.

Finding a space of empathy comes easily to me, but it's harder for me to make a place for anger. To get to a place of forgiveness, I had to get angry and recognize what holding on to the burden I was carrying had cost me. I may not have had the childhood I deserved, but I was tired of carrying that burden and was ready to be free.

A few months after my last session with Daniel, I had a chance to be with my mom for a few days. During our time together, I shared what I had been going through and said the words that I didn't know I needed to say: "I forgive you." Almost immediately thereafter, I started to feel the sense of freedom Daniel had mentioned. And that freedom let me return home to that sensitive little boy I knew long ago and gave me permission to no longer need to be that brave little soldier. I was finally settled.

Journeying On

My hope for readers is that this is just the beginning of a long journey toward finding a sense of calm and settled feelings. As you move down this path, it's important to remember that the journey doesn't have directions that will guide you directly to your destination. You will find your route through your own trials, errors, hardships, and triumphs. Each person you encounter will be a teacher and each day will provide you with experiences that will serve as lessons to shape you and guide you on your way.

Often we look for one source of guidance that will teach us and lead us to where we want to be. We keep searching and putting our faith in teachers, guides, and gurus to save us from our lives and show us the practice or dogma that will lead us home. Although it's important to find people to trust and to open ourselves to new ideas, believing that one person will hold all the answers is flawed and keeps us stuck in unhealthy patterns. What we really need is to open ourselves up to the lessons that are all around us. We need to trust ourselves enough to take the next step forward, knowing that even if we fall, we're still in motion toward where we want to be. The lessons, habits, tools, and meditative practices shared in this book are simply additional sources of inspiration on your journey forward. I encourage you to take what resonates with you and leave behind anything that does not.

Continue to be in motion, continue to trust yourself, continue to find your way back to center even when chaos swirls around you. Remember that your peace is worth fighting for, and *you* are worth the fight.

And when all else fails, take a deep breath in, breathe out, and let it all settle.

About the Author

Michael Galyon has come to be known by many as their compassionate guide on the path to calm. With a kind heart and a deep appreciation for mindfulness, Michael serves as a nurturing presence in the lives of his coaching clients, his 1 million+ social media followers on TikTok (@coachmichael1) and Instagram (@michael.galyon), as well as listeners on his podcast, "Letting It Settle with Michael Galyon." Michael is a certified mindfulness instructor and professional life and business coach credentialed by the International Coach Federation. He is dedicated to creating a safe and inclusive space where individuals can find solace and cultivate a sense of calm amid life's challenges.

With an eclectic background in education, business, the performing arts, and health and wellness, Michael brings a unique perspective to his work and draws on his experience to connect with people from all walks of life. While his work may take him from boardrooms to meditation retreats, his mission remains the same: to help you come home to yourself and find a calmer, kinder, and more connected you.

Read more at michaelgalyon.com.

Index